COLLECTING
FOOTBALL CARDS

Gwendolyn Jahn
February 8, 1999
Thank You God!

COLLECTING FOOTBALL CARDS
A Complete Guide with Prices

MIKE BONNER

WALLACE-HOMESTEAD BOOK COMPANY
Radnor, Pennsylvania

TO CAROL AND KAREN

and

IN MEMORY OF
DAVE KELTS

Published in Radnor, Pennsylvania 19089, by Wallace-Homestead,
a division of Chilton Book Company

Designed by Green Graphics

Cover design by Anthony Jacobson

Manufactured in the United States of America

Library of Congress Cataloging-in-Publication Data
Bonner, Mike, 1951–
    Collecting football cards: a complete guide with prices / Mike
Bonner.
      p.   cm.
    Includes index.
    ISBN 0–87069–737–4 (pb)
    1. Football cards—Collectors and collecting—United States.
2. Football cards—Prices—United States.   I. Title.
GV955.3.B66   1995
796′.49796332′0973—dc20   95–8016
                                                     CIP

1 2 3 4 5 6 7 8 9   4 3 2 1 0 9 8 7 6 5

CONTENTS

CONTENTS
continued

PART 2
SPECIAL CATEGORIES
OF CARDS

PART 3
THE HOBBY OF COLLECTING

PART 4
PRICE GUIDES

ACKNOWLEDGMENTS

My sincere thanks to the many people who helped make this book possible: Jeff Day, Susan Keller, Rebecca Alm, Tucker Freeman Smith, Zachary Reid, Allan Kaye, Tom Hager, Janet Wasko, Carlos Calderon, Dennis Hooker, Alex Corman, Mark Diamone, Steve Galleta, Carl Lamendola, Patrice Donoghue, Randy Hunt, and George Beres.

AN INTRODUCTION TO FOOTBALL CARD COLLECTING

Since 1989 football cards have poured onto the market, fueled by a surge of interest from card collectors around the country. The hobby's current vigor is ironic because until recently football cards existed as poor cousins to baseball cards. Even though the first football cards appeared about the same time as the first baseball cards, they never were as popular as baseball cards and vanished soon after their debut a century ago.

Sports cards themselves owe their existence to competition among tobacco companies in the late 1880s. In those days tobacco firms were in a furious battle to attract customers. Cigarette smoking was considered a manly and rather harmless habit.

Amidst this fierce competition, an unknown marketing genius came up with the idea of increasing cigarette sales by enclosing small cardboard pictures of celebrity and sports figures in cigarette packs.

The idea took off, and soon every tobacco company included cardboard pictures in its cigarette packs. There were pictures of boxers, pool players, singers, musicians, soldiers, vaudeville stars, and football and baseball players, among many others.

The most avidly collected pictures were those of baseball players. Adolescent boys especially seemed to like them. By 1920 several thousand baseball subjects had appeared on cards.

Sports cards owe their existence to competition among tobacco companies in the late 1880s. *Pictured:* 1910 Honus Wagner T-206 tobacco card.

1

Football players were not so lucky. Before 1933 only one set of football player cards existed, the 1890s Mayo set. Because professional baseball had roots in the United States almost from the end of the Civil War, it was a natural for card makers. There was no football equivalent to major league baseball until the early 1920s. The first American professional football league, the National Football League, was founded in 1921, when 13 teams with names like the Canton Bulldogs, the Dayton Triangles, and the Rock Island Independents burst upon a sports-crazed America.

A multisport card set was issued by the Sports Company of America in 1926. It contained cards featuring approximately 30 college football stars and is notable for being the first card set not issued to promote tobacco. The football hobby considers the Sports Company set a minor issue, as the cards feature only West Coast players. The Sports Company cards are scarce and practically unknown to most hobbyists.

It wasn't until 1933, when the Goudey Gum company released another multisport set called the Sport Kings, that football cards reappeared nationally. Three storied football names appear in the Sport Kings set—Red Grange, Knute Rockne, and Jim Thorpe. But with only three football cards among cards for stars of many sports, the Goudey set is by football card standards only a minor set.

A more important set of 36 cards issued by National Chicle Gum appeared two years later. It featured pro football players like Bronko Nagurski, Dutch Clark, Beattie Feathers, and Bernie Masterson, plus a college coach of modest renown, Knute Rockne. The Rockne card is #9 in the National Chicle set.

Sport Kings and National Chicle cards have between them six of the ten most valuable football cards on the market today.

No more football cards were produced until 1948, when chewing gum brands grew popular in the postwar years. From 1948 to the present, at least one football card set has been produced annually. Most years only produced one set; until recently, multiset years in football cards were rare.

Although there seemed to be fertile ground for a new national sport, the NFL struggled in fits and starts before the affluent and leisure-rich 1950s guaranteed success. The 1960s also saw considerable growth in the sport, but profits were small because competition raged between the two major leagues, the AFL and the NFL. Not until the 1970s, when a merger brought an end to the competition, did football begin to supplant baseball as the national passion.

Interest in football cards has followed the slow rise of the sport across the country. Topps Chewing Gum had a monopoly on football cards for 20 years, but when the monopoly finally ended in 1989, a wave of new cards flooded collectors. The backwash from that wave is still with us, and all but the sharpest hobbyists have felt its financially treacherous undertow.

In 1989 the number of major card sets jumped to four. The following year five appeared. The big explosion came in 1991, when 15 sets were issued. In 1992, proving it was no fluke, 20 major nationally distributed sets of pro football cards made it to market.

Football cards have inundated the hobby market in a most remarkable fashion. Today it is a collector's market.

Football cards owe everything to their cousins, baseball cards. Baseball is where it began. But football card collecting has achieved a solid second place, with basketball and hockey cards rising fast. The biggest new customer base for the hobby is men over 30, although the youth market (mainly boys between 6 and 16) is stronger than ever.

Like cards for most pro sports, football cards can be categorized as major or minor. In the football card hobby, major cards and sets are distinguished from minor sets by availability, quality, and collector interest. Major football sets, or "mainstream sets" as they are often called, are the products of companies like Topps Chewing Gum and enjoy nationwide distribution. Minor sets are usually produced by local companies for local fans and collectors, although big companies occasionally make minor sets.

For the convenience of collectors, companies have taken to producing complete "factory sets." A factory set is one of each card issued by a company for players in a particular sport in a particular year. Unlike a "hand set" or a "hand-collated" set, a factory set didn't have to be put together from card packs. The 1991 Score football factory set is a typical example. Score produced one of the most comprehensive sets of football cards ever issued at 690 cards. It cost about $20 originally and came in a brightly decorated cardboard box.

Because of the proliferation of factory sets, you no longer have to trade cards to complete your set in many cases.

As a writer and avid football card collector since the early 1980s, I first produced a piece on the hobby in 1991. Later I was asked to develop a column about football cards for the card hobby monthly *Tuff Stuff*. In writing the column, I sought to present material each month that would illuminate a specific aspect of the hobby, either old or new. By following the columns over a period of time, the reader would have a thorough and accurate picture of the hobby as a whole. My "Gridiron Report" column ended in 1993, although I still contribute occasionally to various sports publications. This book is the culmination of the work I did on the *Tuff Stuff* columns.

To write about football cards effectively, I had to ground myself in the lore of the hobby. As a football fanatic for more than 20 years, I knew about the sport, but I didn't know much about the hobby. Books and magazines containing price guides are handy references, but I wanted to go beyond the set descriptions, fully educating myself in this frequently fascinating, sometimes frustrating field.

Collecting cards is but one of the dozens of collecting hobbies that have modern Americans hooked. Acquiring everything from Hummels to metal lunch boxes has become a national mania. Not for nothing does the bumper sticker say: "He or she who dies with the most stuff wins."

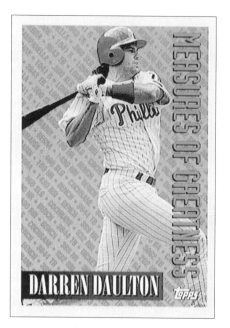

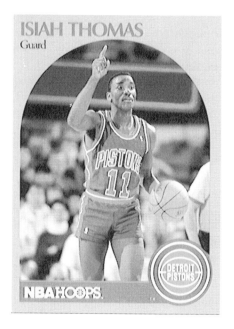

When it comes to collecting, trading cards have most things beat for variety, cost, convenience, and quality. *Pictured, clockwise starting at top left:* 1994 Topps Darren Daulton #608, 1990 NBA Hoops Isiah Thomas #111, 1993 Simpsons SkyBox #53, and 1992 Mother's Cookies Richard Nixon #37.

There are several reasons that sane people would choose to make a hobby of collecting slips of cardboard bearing images of professional athletes and others. Collectors can learn interesting facts, make money, and have something to talk about. The hobby even gives people somewhere to go on the weekends. Card shows are popular in many American cities.

When it comes to collecting, trading cards have most things beat for variety, cost, convenience, and quality.

Besides sports cards, dozens of types of trading cards are being sold. Releases include soap opera stars, musicians, war heroes, cars, motorcycles, cartoon characters, movie and TV spinoffs, animals, politicians, and criminals, to name a few. The subjects suitable for display on trading cards are just about endless. More and more trading cards are being produced, thanks to advances in computerized printing techniques and the peculiar American craving for celebrity mementos. Today it's very much like the days when trading cards first appeared in cigarette packs.

But without the smokes.

The towering figure in the trading card hobby is a man named Jefferson Burdick. He invented the hobby as a hobby, putting together a vast collection of baseball cards and codifying most of the formal terms erudite collectors use to talk shop.

Burdick is known as "the father of card collecting," and his book, *American Card Catalog*, is the classic text on the subject.

Cards featuring sports figures remain the central and most enduring pillar of the trading card industry. Football cards have emerged as a glamour sector of the industry. Baseball, with a long continuous history dating to the tobacco era a century ago, will probably always be the most popular.

But football cards are getting close.

For adults, collecting football cards as investments can be of absorbing interest. While this can (and does) make the hobby profitable for some, the investment can easily go awry, as unlucky collectors who have made poor choices will attest.

It is good to remember what financier Malcolm Forbes said about collecting: "Surround yourself with

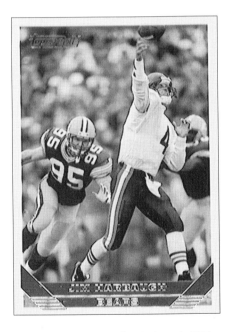

Pictured: **1993 Topps Jim Harbaugh #191.**

the things you love, regardless of investment potential. That way, even if they lose value, you will have nice things."

Buying and selling sports cards is like playing a stock market in human images. Here's how it works: Usually you want to buy the first card issued of a player as a professional. In hobby parlance, that's the rookie card. With luck your player makes it to the championship or performs some other feat of obvious excellence. Now that rookie card you bought early on might be worth hundreds of dollars. Savvy investors can really make a killing.

The trick is that you have to be able to guess which players will have great careers and which ones won't. Not all do.

Another thing that determines value for a card is condition. Collectors are picky about wear. Creases and other defects can drive down the price, even among rarities.

Card centering is another big concern for hobbyists. Many early cards were cut so that the image was shifted to one side or the other of the card face. Fleer football cards of the 1960s are notorious for this problem. A badly centered card is far less valuable than a well-centered card, all other things being equal.

To know football cards, you must know football. Card values are invariably tied up in the career of the

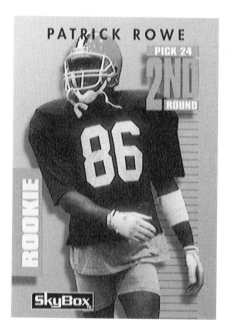

Usually you want to buy the first card issued of a player as a professional—in hobby parlance, the rookie card. *Pictured:* the rookie 1992 PrimeTime Patrick Rowe #133.

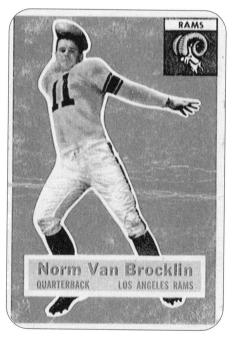

Creases and other defects can drive down prices. *Pictured:* 1956 Topps Norm Van Brocklin #6 with horizontal crease.

player shown on the card. High visibility offensive players like quarterbacks, running backs, and wide receivers are generally more valued than linemen, linebackers, or defensive backs. But there are exceptions.

Another rule of thumb is that old cards are usually more valuable than new cards. Similarly, scarce cards are more valuable than common cards. Exceptions exist to these rules as well.

It is tricky to grasp what makes cards valuable, but there are good reasons to become involved in the hobby besides making money.

Football card collecting can be a lot of fun. A major reason is the wide variety of colorful and extremely intriguing football cards in existence.

Some of the more sought-after cards include the John Dunlop Mayo card, the 1935 National Chicle Nagurski card, the 1952 Bowman Large Lansford card, the 1965 Topps Namath card, and the 1983 Jogo CFL Moon card. Recent items like the Action Packed braille series and the Wild Card stripe series are less costly but no less interesting.

Significant cards and sets abound in the football card hobby. Not only are these cards significant as components of popular culture, but they are also valuable as aids to understanding American obsessions in general.

What do football cards really represent? If you're a follower of sports, cards may be a chance to invest in the career of your hero, if only at the tini-

Card centering is a big concern for hobbyists. *Pictured:* an uncentered 1960 Fleer Bill Krisher #53.

Old cards are usually more valuable than new. *Pictured:* 1935 National Chicle Mike Mikulak #18.

est level. A few collectors follow the career of a single player, seeking out memorabilia for that player alone. Others have broader tastes, chasing cards for a team or a college or yearly sets covering an entire sport.

It is gratifying to note as well that football cards are finally beginning to do justice to a swift, violent sport. The number of players pictured has increased at the same time that design values have vaulted upward. This represents a welcome change from the years up to 1989, before the Topps monopoly ended. Early football cards were mostly crude and poorly designed, and they were few in number. Now even the average player can expect to be pictured on a card during his career, maybe two or three times.

Careers in this high-speed game are short. The chief poet of modern football, Vince Lombardi, saw the game as a place where a man, helped by his comrades, would "run to daylight."

Lombardi's phrase is a simple and powerful evocation of football's near-hypnotic impact on spectators.

The highest honor in professional football is named after Lombardi, the game's greatest coach. Every year the winning Super Bowl team receives the Lombardi Trophy. A chance to participate in football's crowning pageant is the goal every NFL player carries with him on the field. It is the opportunity to become one with the legend of the sport.

The chief poet of modern football was Vince Lombardi. *Pictured:* 1990 Score Vince Lombardi #603.

Football picture cards help us remember the men who have been our gladiators. Formidable and heroic players may live forever in the memory of fans, but it is nice to have a tangible keepsake, however small.

What follows is meant to show the landscape of football cards and, where appropriate, small slices of the game itself.

1

A FOOTBALL CARD CHRONOLOGY

CHAPTER ONE

THE FIRST FOOTBALL CARDS

Stars of the Tobacco Era

The very first football card was issued in 1888 by Goodwin & Company, the makers of Old Judge and Gypsy Queen cigarettes. This original card pictured Henry Beecher, who was then captain of Yale's varsity football squad.

Collector Steve Galletta of Touchdown Cards in New York calls the full-color Beecher card a beautiful collector's item.

"The back is printed in black ink," Galletta said, "and it lists the celebrities included in the Old Judge cards. Most are baseball players, but Buffalo Bill is in there too."

The first complete football card set was issued by the Mayo Cut Plug tobacco company, probably in 1892. The set featured 35 college stars from the "Big Three" football schools of that era—Princeton, Harvard, and

Like their baseball cousins, the first football cards were issued by tobacco makers. *Pictured, from left to right:* Mayo Cut Plug Taylor and Mayo Hickok.

Yale. The cards came in Mayo cigarette packs. With the modern exception of baseball player Lenny Dykstra, you might think sports and tobacco don't mix. But 100 years ago that wasn't true. According to the Census Bureau, the frontier wasn't fully settled until 1890, and the roughhouse habits of smoking and chewing were commonly practiced to a degree unknown today. It must have been pretty miserable for those who were not tobacco users.

Tobacco makers were in a fierce battle for customers. When somebody thought up the idea of adding celebrity picture cards to tobacco pouches and cigarette packs, the idea quickly became popular with youngsters, who collected the cards. Sports figures, especially baseball players, led the way.

Branching out, the Mayo company began including many types of cards with its product. There were cards featuring boxers, pool players, singers, and vaudeville stars, to name a few types. Some of these cards, like the one of boxer John L. Sullivan, are today rare, expensive collectibles.

Mayo's set of cards for 35 college football stars falls in the collectible category. Although it is not known how many original sets exist, the set is without question very rare. It's also hard to say what a complete near-mint set might fetch in the current market, so infrequently is one sold. Probably in the $10,000 to $20,000 range, depending on grade. Formally, it's classified as the P.H. Mayo 302 set.

It has been difficult for even experienced collectors to pin down precisely what year this set was issued. The guides date it 1896. My research on this set indicates that the year of issue probably was 1892, although the first cards in it could have appeared as early as 1889. I base this conclusion primarily on a review of the All-Americans with cards in the set. The majority of All-Americans in the set are clustered in the years 1892–1893, making this period the most probable time of issue. Most likely the cards were issued over several years, as was baseball's 1909–1911 T-206 set. It is likely that we shall never know for certain the first year of issue for this truly historic Mayo set.

The original cards were printed on black cardboard with front photos that are sepia-toned. The solid black backs are blank, without the tobacco advertisements common to later cigarette cards. These cards measure 1⅝" by 2⅞" and are much smaller than modern cards.

A 1990 reprint set is now available to collectors.

The reprint was originated by the late Dennis Eckes from a complete collection. Eckes was a major figure in the sports card collecting hobby whose respect for fact and attention to detail were well-known.

It's encouraging that this significant set is at last available to the average collector. Card dealer Mark Diamone at Discount Dorothy's in Mar Vista, California, says that more attention is now being given to reprint sets.

"Interest in reprints has been stimulated by Topps' success with its Archive baseball set," Diamone says. "One big reason reprints have been slow in coming is that you have to start with a near-mint set, even before you buy the license. Older cards in mint condition are rare enough, let alone a whole set."

A reprint of the Mayo set purchased for $7 at Discount Dorothy's came wrapped in a small clear plastic bag, secured by a piece of tape. The cards themselves are brown on plain white stock with the words "Mayo Cut Plug Football Reprint 1990" on the reverse. They are slightly smaller than the originals with dimensions of 1½" by 2⅝".

The reprint set is a disappointing release for several reasons. First and most important, printing the cards in brown to imitate the original sepia tone just doesn't work. Reprints ought to be as close to the original as possible. On the bottom left of the card fronts, where the Mayo brand and motto is printed, the cheap brown ink bleeds into the white,

making the text unreadable. You may need a magnifying glass to see the Mayo Cut Plug motto.

The lack of original coloring on the backs counts against the reprint too. In some cases, it makes sense to change the backs of tobacco reprint cards. In the Mayo Cut Plug case, a history of the player and career highlights would have been a nice substitution. But like the originals, these cards give no context—just a last name and a school. A checklist and a box to keep the cards in also would have come in handy.

Reprinters would do well to follow the example set by C.C.C. with its excellent T-206 baseball reprint set. The Topps 1953 baseball Archive set is another example of a reprint done right. But this version of the Mayo set is not that special. Should the Mayo set ever again be reprinted, more care needs to be taken with presentation.

Mayo Cut Plug tobacco company issued the first complete football card set. *Pictured, from left to right:* Mayo Butterworth, Mayo Riggs, Mayo Poe.

Apart from the obvious drawbacks of the reprint, though, the Mayo set is worth a close examination. The 35 cards divide into three subsets—Princeton, Harvard, and Yale. The Princeton squad is the best represented, having 13 players. Yale and Harvard both have 11. One card has no school or player name listed.

It's typical that this very first football set contains an error card. Printing errors have plagued the hobby since the beginning, and experience with recent football card sets indicates that the problem is increasing, not decreasing.

The mystery of who is depicted on Mayo card #35 has puzzled collectors for a long time. However, the mystery is at last solved. During my research for this book, I finally uncovered his identity.

The Mayo mystery man was a pi-

The anonymous player on the Mayo Cut Plug 302 set is John Dunlop of Harvard. *Pictured:* Mayo Dunlop.

oneer of the Flying Wedge. Players in the Flying Wedge would surround the ball carrier as he went downfield in a formation not unlike Canadian geese. Practically the only way to disrupt the wedge was to roll into the legs of the blockers or leap over the blockers to get the ball carrier. Serious injuries, such as concussions, were common. The Flying Wedge and other mass momentum plays were banned from football in 1906 at the insistence of President Theodore Roosevelt.

Based on his looks, you might say that the Mayo mystery man was from Harvard. If that was your guess, you would be right. Player #35 on the Mayo Cut Plug 302 set is John W. Dunlop, Class of 1897 and a multisport star at the school.

Card guides like the *Sport Americana* issued by Beckett have always listed the Mayo card #35 as anonymous. In April 1993 I contacted Harvard University archives to see if the picture could be matched to one from Harvard yearbooks of the era. Identical requests went to Yale and Princeton.

At Harvard, curatorial associate Patrice Donoghue graciously searched the records for a match of the player on the anonymous Mayo Cut Plug card and came up with the answer.

Dunlop is positively identified by his picture in *The H Book of Harvard Athletics*, and further confirmation comes through other reference materials on Dunlop.

A winner of four letters in football, Dunlop went on to become a property manager and a partner in his own firm, Sleeper and Dunlop.

Frank Hinkey of Yale was the most memorable player on the Mayo set. *Pictured:* Mayo Hinkey.

After graduation he was a backfield coach at Harvard for two years and later at Holy Cross for one. He died in 1957 at the age of 83.

During the time that players like Dunlop were active, a strong rivalry gripped the schools, each seeking dominance on the playing field. In Allison Danzig's fine history of early football, *Oh, How They Played the Game*, sportswriter Jim Kieran describes early Harvard-Yale contests as slugfests where players emerged "bleeding from cuts or from kicks or smashes in the general mauling."

Primitive football was a game of small imagination, but the spirit of the sport existed right from the start.

The players depicted on the Mayo cards were as close to professionals as the sport then knew. A handful of them are remembered as true legends. End Frank Hinkey of

Yale goes front and center as the most memorable.

Called "The Disembodied Spirit" by contemporary Walter Camp, Hinkey was known for his explosive tackles. George Adee, a Hinkey teammate at Yale, said that Hinkey had "the greatest fighting spirit that ever stepped upon any field."

George Adee is also included among the Yale players in the Mayo set. Like the others, he's dressed in a durable-looking sleeveless leather jerkin, displaying a big "Y" on the left side of his uniform. In the style of the times, his hair is neatly parted down the middle.

Besides Hinkey and Adee, the Mayo set has Princeton stars like captain Jesse Riggs, Thomas "Doggie" Trenchard, and quarterback Edgar Poe. Frank Butterworth of Yale rounds out the list of big names. Win-loss records of the era suggest that the Yale squad was easily the strongest.

Unaccountably missing from the Mayo 302 set is Alonzo Stagg, who was named All-American at end for Yale in 1889, the first of many honors in a long and celebrated football life. As Paul Zimmerman observes in his book *The Thinking Man's Guide to Pro Football*, Stagg was a football pioneer with more than 50 pass patterns in his coaching scheme by 1910. A card showing Stagg in his playing days would have been a treat. Had such a card existed, it would surely be the most valuable card in the hobby.

As history, the Mayo 302 set of football cards is practically incomparable. These cards give a human face to an ancient game. In the formative years of football, rules and scoring

Players like George Adee and Doggie Trenchard are attired in smart period costumes. *Pictured, from left to right:* **Mayo Adee and Mayo Trenchard.**

changed often. Tactics shifted to accommodate the changes. The size and shape of the field were continually debated. The Flying Wedge, the most spectacular of all running plays, was invented in 1892. The forward pass, on the other hand, was decades from perfection. Not until football innovator Walter Camp came along did the game develop into a recognizable version of its present form.

Too bad the Mayo company didn't continue making cards of football players. The 302 set was a first and only, a genuine rookie set. The advent of Buck Duke's American Tobacco monopoly in 1895 put an end to competition in the tobacco industry, thus eliminating the need for premiums.

What collector today could resist a Carlisle Jim Thorpe card, a Pop Warner rookie, or a Fielding Yost? Unfortunately, they were never made. That's the reason football collectors envy the continuous history of baseball cards.

CHAPTER TWO

DEPRESSION-ERA FOOTBALL CARDS

The 1935 National Chicle Gum Set

The two most valuable items in the football card hobby are found in a 36-card set issued in 1935 by the National Chicle Gum Company. In near-mint condition, any one of the common cards may run upwards of $100. The highly sought cards of quarterbacks Bernie Masterson and Dutch Clark also appear in this set, along with such stars as Beattie Feathers, Glenn Presnell, and Clark Hinkle. These cards sell in the $700 to $1,500 range. Many other 1930s stars are somewhere in the middle at $300 to $400. But the two names that stand above all the rest are Bronko Nagurski and Knute Rockne.

The Nagurski and Rockne cards are easily the most coveted specimens the football card hobby has to

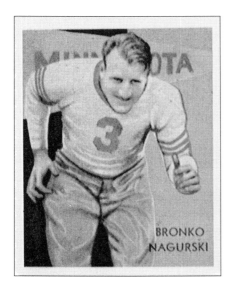
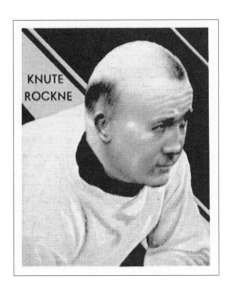

Two names stand above all the rest—Bronko Nagurski and Knute Rockne. *Pictured, from left to right:* **1935 National Chicle Bronko Nagurski #34 and 1935 National Chicle Knute Rockne #9.**

offer. At current prices the Nagurski card, #34 in the set, has a price tag of $9,000, putting it well out of the reach of most collectors. The Rockne card, #9 in the set, is priced at about $3,000.

The availability of this set to the average collector is next to zero. Some dealers have been in business for years without being on the buying or selling end of one of the cards.

Card dealer Dennis Hooker of Hooker's Sports and Collectibles in Oregon says he's been selling football cards full time for six years without coming across an authentic National Chicle card.

"The cards are desirable items," Hooker said. "But as a dealer, I wouldn't be likely to have them. It's not the sort of thing people come in off the street to buy. More likely, a dealer with good contacts would put a buyer and seller together."

Originally packaged with bubble gum in a 1-cent pack, the National Chicle cards are smaller than modern cards, measuring 2½" by 2⅞". They are printed from original oil paintings. The oil paintings were made from line drawings of photographs, exactly like the Topps baseball cards of the early 1950s.

An excellent reprint of the original appeared in 1985 and is still widely available from full-service and mail-order dealers. I purchased mine from Mark Diamone at Discount Dorothy's in Mar Vista, California, for $6.95. Buying reprints like this one is one of the best ways for collectors to absorb hobby lore without going broke.

How does the 1985 reprint set measure up? These cards are great. They're printed on bleached white stock in full color. The graphic style is what people now call art deco, a style popular from the late 1920s to the early 1950s. It features the use of bold color over large areas to highlight realistic detail. Many patriotic posters from the World War II era were done in art deco style.

The names on the Chicle card fronts are lettered in thin, straight lines. It's simple and unadorned with Gothic flourishes. The 1992 Pro Set cards feature a quite pleasing lettering style that is similar to the lettering on the 1935 National Chicle set.

The card backs contain a series of one-paragraph blurbs written by Eddie Casey, coach of the Boston Redskins in 1935. For the most part, the Casey paragraphs are amusing and give the reader some flavor of the

The art deco style of the National Chicle set was a popular form in the 1930s. *Pictured:* 1935 National Chicle Glenn Presnell #5.

Dutch Clark's card is enhanced by Eddie Casey's homespun description on the back. *Pictured:* 1935 National Chicle Dutch Clark #1.

Unfortunately, the printing job on some of the backs is poor, the green ink being too light.

Casey's lines on the cards reveal him to be an astute and articulate observer of the pro game in the 1930s. A good example of Casey's homespun description is his assessment of Mike Mikulak on card #18: "A smart back, like, Mikulak of the Chicago Cardinals, will watch the ball at all times. It is the only way you will get a quick start and that extra split-second advantage that gives you the jump on opposing players."

At the bottom of each card back, two or three short sentences give statistics on the player, including height, weight, and career history. A curious note is the line above the copyright, which states that each player is "one of 240 football players with playing tips." Presumably National Chicle's intentions for the set were more ambitious than the eventual product.

old-time pro game. There is plenty of advice for football novices, with long discussions of running, blocking, tackling, and kicking techniques.

A favorite of many is Shipwreck Kelley. *Pictured:* 1935 National Chicle Shipwreck Kelley #22.

19

A side-by-side comparison between the National Chicle cards and cards issued today is interesting. They're simply not all that different. The text on the solid plastic stock of the 1992 Collector's Edge card of Eagles quarterback Randall Cunningham tells us less about him than that on the cardboard stock used in the National Chicle card of Eagles quarterback Dutch Clark in the 1930s. They played for the Eagles 50 years apart, but Clark had a tendency to hold the ball in a manner very similar to Cunningham's. The Clark card is more informative because of Casey's description. Collector's Edge only gives us Cunningham's picture and some dry statistics. The nod here goes to National Chicle.

Fans and collectors familiar with the conservative style of today's NFL should love the free spirits pictured on the cards in the National Chicle set. There are some fascinating characters—guys with names like Turk Edwards, Glenn Presnell, Dutch Clark, Beattie Feathers, Shipwreck Kelley, and Bo Molenda stand out. A favorite of many is Shipwreck Kelley, a rich Kentuckian who was one of the few player-owners to star in any professional sport.

Kelley had a tough running style and played without a helmet when doing so was still legal. His Brooklyn Dodger football team never fared well, but off the field Kelley thrived in New York café society. It's hard to picture any of the current NFL owners taking their licks by running back punts as Kelley did.

Beattie Feathers is another famous football name ornamenting the National Chicle set. Feathers was a

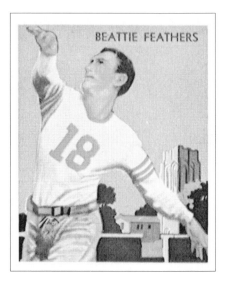

Beattie Feathers was the first 1,000-yard rusher. *Pictured:* 1935 National Chicle Beattie Feathers #23.

rookie for the Chicago Bears in 1934 and became the league's first 1,000-yard rusher. His 1,004 yards were gained on only 101 carries. The Feathers card is #23 in the National Chicle set.

Riding the wings of Feathers, the Bears of 1934 seemed to have a lock on that year's NFL championship. After all, they had ripped through the regular season undefeated for a 13-0 mark. But on came the New York Giants, with a much less impressive 8-5 record. The teams met on an icy field for the crown. Chicago led until halftime, when some of the New York Giants donned sneakers to help them get a footing on the frozen turf.

In short order the Giants turned the famous "Sneakers Game" into a rout, winning 30-13. The most dramatic play in the second half was turned in by Giant back Ken Strong, who scored on a 42-yard run. Strong's card in the National Chicle set is #7.

The Knute Rockne card is an unusual feature of this set. A college coach, Rockne seems out of place in a set of professional players. Yet there he is. His hold on the football imagination was firm even then. Casey describes Rockne as an "immortal of all time" as far as the game is concerned. Casey is no doubt right.

"Immortal" is a good word for Nagurski as well. Through the years Bronko Nagurski has become a synonym for power and strength on the gridiron. That's the reason Nagurski's card is the premier item in the hobby. In his history of Depression-era football, *What a Game They Played,* author Richard Whittingham relates a story by George Halas from Nagurski's rookie season.

After blowing through a pair of tacklers to score a touchdown in Wrigley Field, Nagurski kept right on going, crashing head-on into the brick wall behind the end zone. He fell to the ground, got up, and ran off the field to a worried Halas. Bronk shook his head, saying to Halas:

"That last guy really gave me a good lick, coach."

The year in which the National Chicle cards appeared, 1935, was a pivotal one for the National Football League. The ball had been slimmed down the previous season to modern dimensions. Before 1934 the ball had all the aerodynamic qualities of a watermelon. Quarterbacks and receivers quickly became enamored of the new missile and took to flinging passes all over the field.

At the same time, a player entered the pro game capable of catching those passes, a man with the speed of an antelope who could catch anything thrown from anywhere. His name was Don Hutson and he played for the Green Bay Packers.

On his very first play as a pro, the talented receiver from Alabama raced 83 yards for a touchdown against the Chicago Bears. In Hutson's second season, Green Bay marched effortlessly through the regular season and defeated the Boston Redskins 21-6 in the NFL Championship game.

With Hutson leading the way, Green Bay went on to win a second NFL title in 1939 for Coach Curly Lambeau.

Hutson's career was brand-new when the National Chicle set appeared, and he didn't make it on a card that year. No card appeared for Hutson until a much later decade. Had more pro football cards been issued, Hutson would have been the subject for many.

Another great omission of the period is a card for "Slingin' Sammy" Baugh, the quarterback out of Texas Christian who led the NFL in passing his first season. Baugh had more than 1,100 yards and connected on 14 touchdown passes for the Washington Redskins in 1937, his rookie year.

Redskins owner George Preston Marshall had moved the Redskins out of Boston because of a perceived lack of enthusiasm on the part of Beantown fans. In Washington, D.C., Marshall was more in his element.

Marshall was a great showman who insisted on dressing Baugh in a ten-gallon hat and cowboy boots the first time he met the press, even though Baugh had never before worn either.

With Baugh at the helm, the Redskins tore through the league in 1937, upsetting the Bears in the title game, 28-21.

It's another minor tragedy of the hobby that National Chicle, like its predecessor the Mayo Cut Plug com-

pany, didn't continue making cards at least through the 1930s, before all the best talent went off to war. This 36-card set is just a tiny chronicle of the Depression years in pro football.

Although small, the National Chicle set does credit to the hobby. And unless somebody has money to burn, the 1985 reprint is as close as most of us will get to seeing what the original cards looked like.

CHAPTER THREE

LATE '40s FOOTBALL CARDS

The Leaf and Bowman NFL Sets

As the NFL began to build a following in the late 1930s, World War II suddenly erupted, taking all the best gridiron talent into military service. The league continued to play games throughout the war years, but they were only halfhearted affairs. Manpower was at such a premium in 1943 that the Pittsburgh and Philadelphia teams had to be combined in a hybrid team known as the Phil-Pitt "Steagles."

World War II didn't just drain off the best players. It took coaches, promotional personnel, and fans away from the game, some forever. All told, more than 600 NFL players served in the military during the war. Twenty-one lost their lives.

Not surprisingly, no football cards appeared during the war years. It wasn't until 1948, when new chewing gum brands became popular, that football cards again came on the scene.

Both the Bowman and Leaf com-

Notre Dame's Johnny Lujack served in the Navy. *Pictured:* 1948 Bowman Johnny Lujack #3 front and reverse.

panies produced card sets for the 1948 autumn campaign in the National Football League. The Bowman and Leaf football cards were packaged one card and one stick of gum to every 1-cent pack. To properly evaluate the sets, it is best to examine them together, since they are similar in many respects and were issued the same year.

But the pioneering Leaf and Bow-man sets do differ in several important areas. And of the two 1948 sets, the cards made by Leaf are the more distinctive.

There are 98 football cards in the 1948 Leaf set. The player pictures on the front have monochrome flesh areas and solid color backgrounds. The cards are not quite square, measuring 2⅜" by 2⅞". Up against modern cards they seem small and thin, be-

The 1948 Bowman set features storied names like Sammy Baugh, Charlie Conerly, and Bob Waterfield. *Pictured, clockwise from top right:* 1948 Bowman Sammy Baugh #22, 1948 Bowman Bob Waterfield #26, and 1948 Bowman Charlie Conerly #12.

ing made of gray or cream card stock of low quality. The design is also bad and the printing job substandard.

Offsetting these generally poor features is the huge array of great players getting their first exposure on a card. Like the companion 1948 Bowman set, the Leaf cards feature storied football names like Sammy Baugh, Sid Luckman, Doak Walker, Charlie Conerly, and Bob Waterfield.

The list of big names translates into major value. By 1994 the price of the Leaf set in near-mint condition was close to the cost of an economy car, about $7,000.

Oddly enough, the 1948 Bowman set sells at a small step above that level, $7,500. Though it lacks color, the Bowman set sells for more because it has ten more cards. Either set is extremely rare in near-mint condition, and because they appear so early in the hobby, they are no doubt worth the high prices they command.

Unfortunately, a big hole in the Bowman set holds it back. For whatever reason, the 1948 Bowman has no card for Detroit Lion quarterback Bobby Layne.

Layne was not only a great player but also a legendary figure in the game. Had there been an annual award for the player most admired by peers, Layne would have been a shoo-in. He was a special kind of individual.

Other than the Layne omission, the 1948 Bowman set is strong. All 108 cards are monochrome photos and text on white card stock. The lack of color weakens it considerably, a problem Bowman corrected in 1950 with its second major football

set. Like the Leaf cards, the Bowman set is small and squarish, measuring 2$\frac{1}{16}$" by 2$\frac{1}{2}$".

Will the Bowman set increase in value by the turn of the century? At present rates, it probably will, making today's price for a near-mint set seem like a bargain. A 100 percent increase in value by year 2000 is a real possibility. If Layne had been in the cards, there's no telling where the set might go.

How about the 1948 Leaf set? Will it go up? The obvious key here is the inclusion of Layne in the Leaf set. Another is Leaf's crude though effective use of color. So in terms of selection and design, Leaf bettered Bowman. The only boast 1948 Bowman could make was being first on the field, appearing in stores a few months before the Leaf cards.

The printing techniques available at the time were nothing compared to what is now available. Most newspapers after World War II still used linotype, a process that involved molding hot lead for every letter. It's easy to excuse the poor quality of the Bowman set, although it is ironic to note that the 1935 National Chicle set, printed more than a dozen years earlier, has higher production values and colored artwork.

The best thing about the Leaf and Bowman card sets is the wide array of football superstars pictured. Besides quarterbacks like Bobby Layne, Sid Luckman, Sammy Baugh, Bob Waterfield, and Charlie Conerly, the Leaf set holds the first card of Philadelphia Eagle Chuck Bednarik.

Bednarik was one of the last "60 minute" men in the league, a guy who starred on offense and defense by playing at center and linebacker.

A throwback to the era of 24-man rosters, Bednarik personally handed Green Bay Packer coach Vince Lombardi his only loss ever in a contest for the NFL crown. Bednarik's feat in the 1960 NFL Championship game came on the final play when Bednarik stopped Packer fullback Jim Taylor nine yards short of a winning score.

An exceptionally high caliber of players poured into NFL teams in the years right after the war. Returning veterans enrolled in college in massive numbers because of the GI Bill, swelling the ranks of varsity teams across the country. Once out of school, these men were not typical college grads. Tempered by the war and determined to succeed, they brought a new style to professional football.

The NFL quickly drew on this new pool of talent to produce some of the most exciting players and teams the sport has yet seen. One of these players, Norm Van Brocklin, summed up their attitude by saying: "Playing professional football is one of the hardest ways there is to make easy money."

In a separate but related 1946 development, the NFL also ended the formal color line by signing UCLA star Kenny Washington to the Los Angeles Rams. He is the first African-American player to appear on a nationally marketed NFL football card. Unlike baseball, football has traditionally favored ability first.

It's inspiring to see Kenny Washington in both the 1948 Leaf and Bowman football card sets. He

The NFL broke the color line by signing UCLA star Kenny Washington to the Rams. *Pictured:* 1948 Bowman Kenny Washington #8.

doesn't get the full treatment players like Rocket Ismail and Deion Sanders would rate today, but he comes close.

Washington is #8 in the 1948 Bowman set and #17 in the 1948 Leaf set. Washington's card in the Leaf set also happens to contain a rare variation of the type that sets hearts of football card collectors aflutter. This variation means there are two Kenny Washington cards in the Leaf set: #17A and #17B.

On Leaf #17A Washington's name is printed in white ink on the card front; on #17B it's in black. There is no known reason for the variation. At any rate, both are a bargain at under $100.

A drawback to both sets is that they feature no players from the All-American Football Conference. In the late 1940s, the AAFC was a serious competitor to the NFL. Three clubs that exist today are descended from the eight-team AAFC—the San Francisco 49ers, the Indianapolis (then Baltimore) Colts, and the Cleveland Browns.

The Cleveland Browns were the titans of the AAFC, winning all four championships. Under the guidance of coach Paul Brown, the team favored an all-out passing attack. Otto Graham, a player from Northwestern, was chosen by Brown as quarterback. Soon the Browns were running up huge leads over their AAFC opponents, and Brown's coaching ability became widely recognized.

Swallowing up a rival league is a time-honored tradition for the NFL. Over the years the league has successfully added veteran expansion teams to its ranks by this technique. It worked well in 1950 with the AAFC and again in the 1960s with the American Football League. It has failed only once. In 1986 an adverse court decision meant that real estate magnate Donald Trump couldn't force his USFL New Jersey Generals into the league.

Having cards for AAFC players from the four years that the upstart league existed would be great. Sadly, there aren't any.

Still, the charm of the Bowman and Leaf 1948 sets remains undiminished. The Leaf set especially has within it the magic of 1940s football, which can be summed up in two words: Bobby Layne.

The rookie card of Detroit's answer to Sammy Baugh is #6 in the 1948 Leaf set, #67 in the 1949 Leaf set. Layne is undoubtedly one of most colorful football players of all time.

He hails from the era, it is said, when men were men and women were glad of it. Although he was as dedicated to winning as later, more conventional players like Roger Staubach, Layne darted through the night like a professional lounge lizard. Out on the field, though, it was a different story. There Layne was tough and displayed eptional courage.

A famous photograph of Layne from late in his career shows him ready to take a snap from center. His line is in the set position, man after man in the Lions silver and blue. All of the players in the photo wear face guards on their helmets—all except the reckless Layne.

Ironically, Layne missed out on what should have been his supreme personal moment as quarterback for the Detroit Lions. After leading the Lions into the 1957 Championship game, an injured Layne had to sit on the sidelines while his backup, Tobin Rote, threw four touchdown passes en route to a 59-14 drilling of the Cleveland Browns.

In 1949 only Leaf made football cards. Bowman missed the boat entirely. Leaf issued a small skip-numbered set similar to its baseball cards of the period. The 1949 Leaf cards began with #1 and ended with #150, although no cards existed for a majority of the intermediate numbers. The set is rare but not nearly as interesting for collectors as Leaf's 1948 set because it lacks rookie cards. That omission seriously depresses the value of this second, smaller set. Collectors say that since all the players pictured are already in the 1948 Leaf football set, the 1949 set is nothing special. Since collectors have judged it inferior, the 1949 Leaf set has a relatively low price of $1,500.

Both Leaf and Bowman left a lasting heritage to the hobby by issuing football card sets in 1948. Football card collectors can also be grateful that Leaf followed up with a 1949 set, however small and unambitious it may have been.

Never mind that the design and printing of these sets are poor and color all but absent. At least these historically significant cards exist, and today they are highly sought collectibles in America's favorite sport.

CHAPTER FOUR

EARLY '50s FOOTBALL CARDS

Bowman's String of Classic Sets

The word "classic" gets thrown around a lot in popular culture. There are "classic" television shows, movies, books, cars, games, comics, fashions, and art objects. There is even a "classic" soda pop—Coke Classic.

Every once in a while there's an instance in which the word might actually apply. It just might apply to Bowman's NFL football card lineup from 1950 to 1955.

Bowman Gum Company of Philadelphia got into the football trading card market in 1948 with a 108-card set. At the same time, Leaf issued a 98-card NFL set that boasted two colors, in contrast to Bowman's black-and-white. In 1949 Leaf was the sole manufacturer of NFL football cards, issuing an odd, extremely rare 49-card set. In style and content, it's a reprise of Leaf's numerically larger 1948 set.

In 1950 Bowman came roaring back with a brilliantly colored set containing 144 cards. This set is loaded with Hall of Fame–caliber players and is the defining Bowman football card release of the early postwar period. It is available as a reprint.

Bowman's 1950–1955 lineup was classic. *Pictured:* 1950 Bowman Bobby Layne #37.

The cards are slightly undersized by today's standards, shaped more like squares than rectangles. However, the colors really set them off, with player pictures that look like tiny oil paintings. The backs feature Five Star Collector's Club logos and brief player biographies.

Among the Hall of Fame rookies in Bowman's 1950 set are Lou "The Toe" Groza, Marion Motley, Otto Graham, and Y. A. Tittle. Of all the players in the 1950 set, Motley would probably stack up best against modern athletes. He played fullback for Cleveland in 1950 as the combination Emmitt Smith/Thurman Thomas of his day. A big back at 238 pounds with great speed, Motley was underused in the Brown's attack, but he managed to make All-Pro in 1950 anyway as the league's leading rusher.

The 1951 Bowman set is a personal favorite. Again it contains 144 cards, and it has a format similar to Bowman's 1951 baseball release. The cards are slightly larger than those of the 1950 set, just a hair less than modern size. The backs have maroon ink on gray stock. Combined with the gorgeously colored and dramatically shaded front pictures, the colors of the backs have great eye appeal.

The text on the back of each card is written in that wholly charming Tonto School of Sports Description. Take, for example, Norm Van Brocklin's 1951 rookie: "Led National Football League in passing in 1950. All Pacific Coast in 1948. Joined Rams in 1949. Noted for coming through to win games in the pinch."

You have to love a writing style that can sum up the Dutchman's first two years in the NFL in exactly 27 words.

Bowman's dual sets of 1952 cards

Among the Hall of Fame rookies in the 1950 Bowman set are Y. A. Tittle and Otto Graham. *Pictured, from left to right:* **1950 Bowman Y. A. Tittle #5 and 1950 Bowman Otto Graham #45.**

Of all the players in the 1950 Bowman set, Marion Motley would stack up best against modern players. *Pictured:* 1950 Bowman Marion Motley #43.

the Lansford card is already the third most valuable football card in the hobby. Had Lansford been anything more than an ordinary player, this card could well be in the throes of the speculative fever that has lately driven the Topps baseball Mickey Mantle card of the same year right through the roof.

Adding shine to the 1952 set is the rookie card of Frank Gifford. Others of note are Art Donovan, Yale Lary, Andy Robustelli, and Hugh "The King" McElhenny.

After 1952 the Bowman product fell off considerably. The 1953 release continues the large size but has fewer cards, and it seems as if the creative steam simply dissi-

are the peak football effort by the company. It doesn't matter why the company issued complete, otherwise identical 144-card large and small sets that year. What matters is that the 1952 Bowman large set is now a "Holy Grail" of the hobby. Recently listed at $12,000 in the guides, it rivals and may eventually surpass the legendary National Chicle set in value.

What makes the 1952 Bowman large set so desirable?

First, the cards measure 2½" by 3¾"—a good-sized piece of cardboard. Bowman printed far fewer of these larger cards than it did of their smaller brothers. By one of those quirks that quicken the pulse of collectors, the last card in the set, Jim Lansford of the Dallas Texans, seems to have been printed hardly at all. With a near-mint price tag of $2,800,

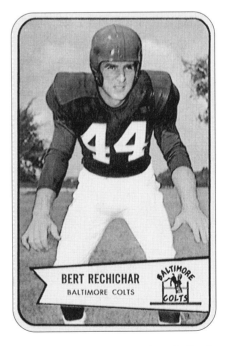

After 1952 the Bowman product declined. *Pictured:* 1954 Bowman Bert Rechichar #26.

pated. Perhaps the cost of producing large and small sets in 1952 exhausted the company. There's a subtle shift to straight photography on the card fronts, and the pennants with player names were replaced in 1953 by a simulated football way too large for the small printed name within.

In 1954 Bowman boosted production to 128 cards but again reduced the quality of the set. All of the player pictures are photographs—some of them quite poor. Nearly any likeness of a player was deemed satisfactory. The only notable rookie card in the 1954 Bowman set belongs to George Blanda, who was then quarterbacking the Chicago Bears. Bowman caught him at the dawn of a career that spanned the better part of three decades.

The 1955 set was the swan song for Bowman. Here at last some of the old energy returns to the design. This is also the largest of Bowman's seven football card releases, with a total of 160 cards. Like the others, it's a little weak on rookies, a problem common to football card sets before the 1980s. Pat Summerall, better known to modern fans as a broadcaster than as a player, claims the top rookie spot in the 1955 set. Nevertheless, this final Bowman effort was good enough to be copied by Topps, setting football card standards for the rest of the decade.

Topps purchased Bowman Gum in January 1956, beginning a produc-

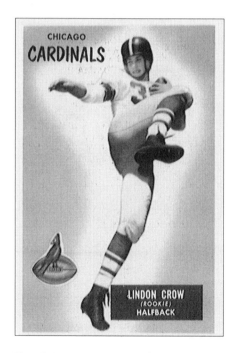
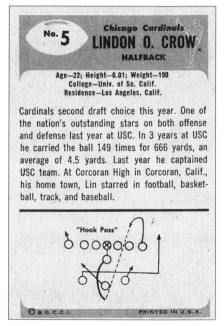

The 1955 Bowman set was that company's swan song. *Pictured:* **1955 Bowman Lindon Crow #5 front and reverse.**

tion schedule that has lasted nearly 40 years.

Dealer John Montgomery is adept at putting together sets of vintage Bowman football cards and regularly sells them from his business, Colorado Cards, based in Evergreen. He says, "I consider the early Bowman football sets attractively priced and an excellent investment."

How good an investment are the early Bowman football sets? The numbers tell the story. A study of old price guides reveals that the value of the 1952 large set has increased from about $7,000 in 1990 to about $12,000 in 1993.

Stockbrokers will tell you that any investment ballooning in value 71 percent over a three-year period is more than just excellent.

Professional football in the 1950s had an exuberance lost in the money-grubbing atmosphere that now surrounds the sport. In those days players knew that what they were doing wasn't all that important. For many of them, a football career was nothing more than a lark, a post-college diversion like a trip to Europe. The Bowman football cards give collectors some of the flavor of that era in sport.

It was indeed a special era in the history of football. In 1950, when NFL commissioner Bert Bell announced the merger of the National Football League and the All-American Football Conference, five of the eight AAFC teams did not make the cut. The three that did were the Cleveland Browns, the San Francisco 49ers, and the Baltimore (now Indianapolis) Colts.

With the Cleveland Browns, the AAFC submitted an instant contender for the NFL crown. Fans of the AAFC didn't have to wait long for Paul Brown's team to prove its prowess against the more highly regarded NFL teams.

Although the AAFC was considered an inferior league, Paul Brown's Browns were not an inferior team. They went through the regular season without much trouble, posting a 10-2 mark, tied for best with the powerful New York Giants. Then, in what must have been a hugely satisfying experience, the Browns defeated the Giants 8-3, earning the right to meet the Los Angeles Rams for the league title.

Many since have argued that the Browns vs. Rams 1950 NFL Championship game was perhaps the most exciting ever played. It was finally decided when Lou Groza booted a field goal for the Browns to win it, 30-28.

From that point on, the Browns were a major force in the NFL, appearing in the next five NFL Championship games and winning two of them.

Bowman's football cards catch this remarkable team at its height. Outstanding passer Otto Graham is featured on card #2 in both the 1951 and the 1952 Bowman sets. Coach Paul Brown even qualifies for his own card, #14 in the 1952 double set. The Brown coach card is quite a worthwhile catch for collectors, although other coach cards in the 1952 large set are more valuable because they are scarce short prints. Scarcity accounts for the high value placed on the large set's Joe Stydahar coach card, which is priced on the hobby market at about $450.

The true definition of the word "classic" is one of a kind, or the standard by which others are measured. The Bowman cards of the 1950s could have been better in some respects, but as far as the hobby is concerned, they are pretty good. For their timeless color and quality, they deserve to be called classic.

CHAPTER FIVE

TOPPS GOES INTO FOOTBALL CARDS

Five Sets From the Late 1950s

After Topps Chewing Gum purchased competitor Bowman in 1956, the company was faced with a dilemma. How should it proceed with Bowman's NFL contract? Although Topps had established itself as the dominant maker of baseball trading cards, it had little experience in football cards. The underlying problem was that while Topps now owned Bowman, the football card contract was between the NFL and Bowman, not Topps. The new owners had no authority to issue football cards without first obtaining an agreement with the NFL.

Sy Berger, a Topps executive, got in touch with Bert Bell, then the NFL commissioner. Berger and Bell established a rapport lasting until Bell's death in 1959.

The football card contract problems were resolved when Berger got Commissioner Bell to agree to a new contract. The idea was to use the cards to promote NFL football, and Topps would share the profits with the league. But would the money go to the league or directly to the players? Eventually, it was decided that royalties from the Topps series of football trading cards would go into a player pension fund, to be administered by Bell.

How card companies gain the rights to player images has changed substantially over the years. In the 1950s player images and team emblems were licensed out by the league to companies such as Topps and Bowman.

Today the situation is far more complex. Star players with top agents are often allowed to market their independent images directly to different card companies. These companies compete to sign players to exclusive contracts. Lesser players lack the clout to demand special treatment. In most cases player images are licensed to card companies through league marketing vehicles that also control merchandising for a variety of other official products. In the NFL the agency for this activity is NFL Properties Inc.

Nevertheless, it remains the province of about 100 top-flight stars and rookies to sell their images to some card companies over others. This leads to endless debates about the superiority of player selection

35

from one set to another. In the innocent era known as the 1950s, football cards weren't the cutthroat business proposition they are now.

Thus it was that Bell and Berger began negotiations informally. "Bell and I had similar ideas about using the cards as a promotion for the league," Berger said later. "He was eager to do it in a way that would also make a profit for Topps."

There still remained the question of what kind of cards to produce, how many, and which players to spotlight. Topps opted for the conservative approach.

Instead of trying to break new ground, Topps chose to stick with the Bowman formula. There were to

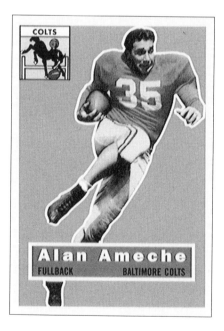

In the first years after buying Bowman, Topps decided to stick with Bowman's formula for producing and designing football cards. *Pictured:* 1956 Topps Alan Ameche #12.

be only minor alterations. At the time, it made sense for Topps to take this approach.

Aside from a couple of experimental collegiate sets in the early 1950s, all Topps had to its credit in football cards was the 100-card 1955 Topps All-American set. While that set is highly significant to collectors, it must not have been a strong seller because Topps never attempted another similar set.

The 1955 Topps All-American set is a landmark because it features 100 of the most storied names in the history of the college game. It includes Knute Rockne, Pudge Heffelfinger, Red Grange, Jim Thorpe, and Alonzo Stagg, among others. With cards slightly larger than modern ones, the All-American set was a promising beginning for Topps. The design work is smoothly done and the cards have an uncluttered, bright, and attractive look. It is delightful to see cards devoted to the Four Horsemen, Red Grange, Iowa hero Niles Kinnick, and Jim Thorpe.

Jim Thorpe's contribution to the development of football, both personal and professional, is practically without equal. While others brought attention and innovation to the sport, Thorpe brought the fans. He was football's first true superstar—a player who could run, kick, block, tackle, and throw. Don't even try to imagine the kind of money a player of Thorpe's ability would command today.

Carrying Thorpe's likeness makes card #37 in the 1955 Topps All-American set worth about $300. This is nearly the best football card in existence for this remarkable athlete, second only to the classic 1933 Goudey Thorpe card. Listed in the price guides at 10 percent of the full set's value, the Thorpe card is a bargain. The entire 100-card set is also low-priced at about $3,000. This is another case where the exact value is hard to pin down as the set is rarely available for sale.

Probably the most famous Thorpe story concerns his play in an early professional game between the Canton Bulldogs and the Massillon Tigers. Thorpe was the star player for the Bulldogs. Knute Rockne, later to coach at Notre Dame, was a defensive end for the Tigers.

Rockne had tackled Thorpe for losses on two successive plays. The second time around, Thorpe is said to have told Rockne: "You shouldn't do that, Rock. All these people came out to see Jim run."

"Well, go ahead and run," Rockne answered. "If you can."

On the very next play, Thorpe burst over the middle, trampling Rockne on his way to a long touchdown. Afterward, Thorpe congratulated Rockne.

"Nice going, Rock," he said. "You sure let old Jim run that time."

Little of the pizzazz from the Topps All-American set shows up in the 1956 regular set of professional players. There is only one innovation: team cards. Otherwise it's a dull set that looks at first glance like a copy of the 1955 Bowman cards. Closer examination, however, reveals a few differences.

At 120 cards, the Topps 1956 set has fewer cards than the 1955 Bowman, but it includes an unnumbered checklist. The checklist is the scarcest

of all the 1956 Topps cards and sells for $350 in near-mint condition.

Finding an early checklist in near-mint is almost impossible because early collectors (mostly kids) had an annoying habit of using a checklist as a checklist! They went through their little piles of cards and marked off names and numbers of the cards they owned. Often they used ink to make these marks. Ink or pencil—whatever the tool—the result is the same: A marked checklist is a ruined checklist.

Topps also changed the orientation on the card backs and the position of the logos on the fronts. The Bowman 1955 cards have card backs set vertically; the Topps cards are horizontal. The 1955 Bowman cards have team logos in the lower right; the 1956 Topps cards have them in the upper right. Card size is also slightly different, with the Topps cards ⅛" larger than the Bowman 1955 set.

But that's about it for differences. In 1956 Topps decided to stick with Bowman's successful design formula, avoiding any changes that might offend collectors. Probably few noticed the company making the cards had changed. What they were even less likely to notice was a change in the flavor of the gum.

Trading card gum is only good when it's fresh. And it's hardly ever fresh.

By 1957 Topps felt comfortable enough in the business of selling football cards to stretch itself a bit. The 1957 set jumps to 154 cards, with not one but two unnumbered checklists. The card fronts have a split picture with a posed action shot next to a head-and-shoulders portrait. The

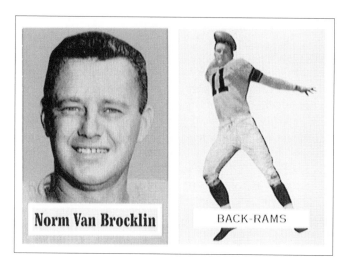

Big-time stars like Norm Van Brocklin make the 1957 Topps set a hot one for collectors.

card backs are printed in red and black on gray card stock.

Big-time rookie cards make the Topps 1957 set a hot one for collectors. Johnny Unitas, Bart Starr, and Paul Hornung all appear for the first time on football cards in 1957.

Another solid card is #85, Dick "Night Train" Lane, then a Chicago Cardinal rookie but later a great cornerback with the Detroit Lions.

Detroit has always had luck with defensive backs. In the 1950s it was Night Train. Later on it was the great Lem Barney. More recently, it has been heavy hitter Bennie Blades.

The best set of the early Topps era is the 1958 set. Topps went with a rounded portrait design on the card fronts, and it works. The set contains 132 cards, the equivalent of a full cardboard sheet. As a result, there are no short-printed cards, a welcome relief from one of the aggravations dogging collectors of early football cards.

Short-printed cards are cards that

were printed less often. This would happen when the company printed cards on more than one sheet of cardboard. Not enough were left to fill the second sheet, so extras were printed from the first sheet. By the time the print run was complete, some cards were more and some less abundant.

Short prints were regularly a problem for collectors who bought cards in the late 1950s. Often a collector would accumulate two copies of one card, three of another, and none of what was really wanted. Pure luck dictated whether the set got filled. Short prints are a great headache for collectors.

The 1958 set is a pleasant exception to the short print plague. Like the 132-card Topps USFL sets the company produced almost 30 years later, the 1958 Topps set was printed on a single full 132-card sheet. Why Topps didn't stick with the full sheet is a mystery.

Another major plus for the 1958

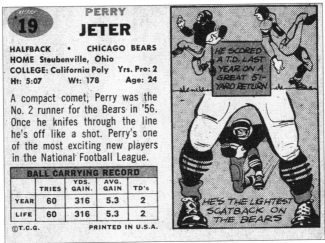

Pictured: **1957 Topps Perry Jeter #19 front and reverse.**

Topps set is the rookie card of Cleveland running back Jim Brown. At $500 or more, the Brown card accounts for a full third of the set's total value.

Brown is a football legend who deserves to have a rookie card in the value stratosphere. In nine years as a running back, Brown collected a bunch of rushing titles, including five in his first five years. Brown's 12,312 career rushing yards stood atop the league for two decades, until the record was broken by the durable and determined Walter Payton of the Chicago Bears in 1984.

On the downside, the 1958 Topps set marks the first appearance of the

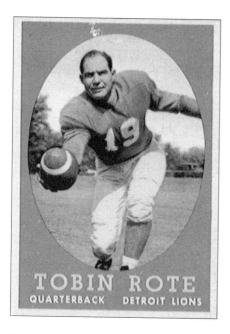

TOBIN ROTE
QUARTERBACK   DETROIT LIONS

ZEKE BRATKOWSKI
QUARTERBACK   CHICAGO BEARS

Topps' 1958 set is a pleasant exception to the short print plague that made collecting an entire set of cards so difficult in the 1950s. *Pictured:* 1958 Topps Tobin Rote #94.

Player names in the 1959 Topps set are printed in a hokey two-color scheme that looks awful. *Pictured:* 1959 Topps Zeke Bratkowski #90.

dreaded scratch-off quiz on the card backs, a card-wrecking device if ever there was one.

In 1959 Topps went without a competitor for the last time until the late 1960s. The 1959 Topps set has 176 cards, the largest of the "Fabulous '50s" football sets. This is the second time Topps offered a scratch-off quiz.

The 1959 set is printed on white stock with gray ink on the back. On the front the player names are printed in a hokey two-color scheme that looks awful. The big rookie in this set is Alex Karras, although Packer coach Vince Lombardi's literary Boswell, Jerry Kramer, is in here too.

Kramer's books about his days

with the Packers, *Instant Replay* and *Farewell to Football,* show him to be a sensitive and articulate man. On balance, Kramer admired Lombardi, especially his motivational skills. Not everyone shares Kramer's high opinion of Lombardi, although nearly everyone acknowledges Lombardi's contribution to the pro game.

Overall, Topps did an adequate job of producing football cards during its years alone in the late 1950s, when it first monopolized the card market for football. But adequate is about all that you can say about the Topps product. It took a second company and a new league to shake up football cards forever. By 1960 big changes were in the making.

CHAPTER SIX

TOPPS vs. FLEER, 1960–1963

First Era of Competition

Topps Chewing Gum had the pro football card market all to itself from 1956 to 1959, and its effort in that period was marked by a series of uninspired NFL football card releases.

But in 1960 everything suddenly changed. A group of wealthy businessmen, calling themselves the "Foolish Club" and chaired by former Marine aviator Joe Foss, founded the new American Football League. Teams were located in Boston, Buffalo, Dallas, Denver, Houston, Los Angeles, New York, and Oakland. The league began an immediate search for talent to fill the rosters. By the fall of 1960, they were ready to play.

At the same time, Fleer threw down a similar challenge to dominant football card maker Topps. That came when Fleer issued a 132-card AFL football set in 1960.

The quality of football cards increased sharply during the four years of Topps/Fleer competition in the early 1960s. This improvement stems in part from advances in printing techniques, but mostly it can be traced to attempts by the two companies to outdo each other. The competition made for an exciting era in the history of football cards and directly benefited collectors.

West Coast card dealer Dennis Hooker of Hooker's Sports and Collectibles notes that early 1960s cards

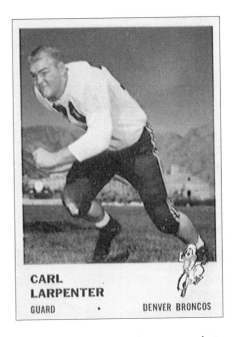

CARL
LARPENTER
GUARD • DENVER BRONCOS

The early 1960s Fleer cards are somewhat hard to find. *Pictured:* 1961 Fleer Carl Larpenter #150.

are relatively scarce and underpriced in the guides.

"The early 1960s cards are somewhat hard to find and can usually command prices in excess of Beckett's, depending on condition. High-grade cards are almost nonexistent, especially among the rarer issues, like the 1963 Fleer set."

Jim Beckett's *Football Card Monthly* and Beckett's annual *Sport Americana Football Card Price Guide* are two leading national football card price compendiums. More dominant in the past, Beckett is now being challenged by a plethora of new guides. But for the purpose of studying 1960s football sets, Beckett is still the authority.

The sets produced by Fleer and Topps during their rivalry in the 1960s illustrate how competition tends to improve quality.

The 1960 Fleer AFL football set contains 132 cards. The price for the set is now $600 to $700 chiefly because it contains an authentic "star" card—the rookie card of then–Los Angeles Charger quarterback Jack Kemp. Later on, Kemp also had some success in the political arena. The Kemp card represents about half the set's value, selling alone in near-mint condition for about $300.

The design of the 1960 Fleer cards is solid, and the selection of players in addition to Kemp is also good. The card fronts are full color, and the card backs are printed in red and black ink on white stock.

Another notable card from the set belongs to iron man George Blanda, who revived a flagging career by joining the Houston Oilers. Discarded by the NFL Chicago Bears,

Blanda went south, giving the Oilers four solid years at quarterback in a career lasting another 15 years.

In one exceptional AFL game, Blanda threw 68 passes against the Buffalo Bills, connecting on 37 of them. The Blanda card is the second most valuable card in the 1960 Fleer set, although it is only one-tenth as costly as Kemp's at $30 to $35.

Just about the only problem with the 1960 Fleer set is the centering of the cards. Poor quality control led to many badly centered cards, placing the picture too near the card edge.

Strictly on the basis of design, the 1960 Topps NFL set does not measure up to the Fleer set of the same year. Like the Fleer set, it contains 132 cards and sells in the $600 to $700

On the basis of design, the 1960 Topps NFL set does not measure up. *Pictured:* 1960 Topps Ralph Guglielmi #123.

range today. But there the similarity ends.

The 1960 Topps set is known for the famous football names it contains, although it does not have the equivalent of the Fleer set megastar, Jack Kemp. It does have Johnny Unitas, Jim Brown, Bart Starr, Paul Hornung, and Frank Gifford. Significantly, all these Hall of Fame players have their rookie cards in earlier sets. The key rookie card in the 1960 Topps set is #57, Forrest Gregg, an All-Pro guard for the Green Bay Packers and later coach of the Cincinnati Bengals.

The 1960 Topps set is marred by a "Football Funnies" scratch-off quiz on the card backs, the major card-wrecking device of the period. The card fronts are borderless, and player names are displayed within an oversized football. As a design gimmick, the old "name in the big football" was trendy when Bowman first did it in 1953. But by 1960 the concept was stale.

Overall, the Topps NFL effort in 1960 has to be termed poor. It was made to look even worse by the clean, strong design of Fleer's 1960 AFL football release. Had it not been for the great players Topps pictured in its cards that year, the 1960 set would be entirely forgettable.

In 1961 both Topps and Fleer produced card sets that featured players from both the AFL and the NFL. The year 1961 marked a high point in the rivalry of the two gum companies for the loyalty of football card collectors.

The competition between Topps and Fleer presented the NFL and the AFL with a rare opportunity to cash in on a licensing bonanza. This was the only time in football card history that two rival leagues sold card licenses to rival companies in the same year.

Many good and bad things can be said about each of the sets. The 1961 Topps set is again hurt by a scratch-off quiz on the card backs. The card backs are printed in light blue ink,

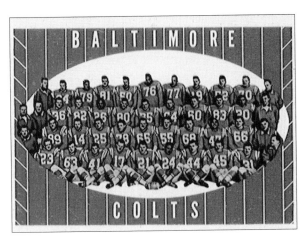

The 1961 Topps set contains AFL and NFL players and teams. *Pictured:* 1961 Topps Baltimore Colts (of the NFL) #9.

and there are a total of 198 cards in the full set. The 198-card total includes three numbered checklists.

Strangely absent in this 1961 Topps set are big-time rookie cards, with the possible exception of San Francisco quarterback John Brodie. The only other rookie cards of note are Tom Flores, Jim Otto, and Don Maynard. All three were fine players of genuine talent, but none are in a class with players like Jim Brown, Paul Hornung, or Johnny Unitas, at least not as far as collectors are concerned. The lack of such star material keeps down the price of a complete 1961 Topps set, which today sells for just a $1,100 in near-mint condition.

The card fronts in the 1961 Topps set are mostly posed photographs of players on the sidelines or at practice. The player photos are clear, the focus is sharp, and the color is good. The front pictures are the best part of a set mostly long on bad and short on good.

The 1961 Fleer football card set also features players from both the NFL and AFL. It certainly was a vintage year for football cards. The Fleer set weighs in at 220 cards, giving collectors in that first year of the Kennedy administration more than 400 pro football cards to choose from.

Unlike the 1961 Topps set, the Fleer set has an authentic superstar in #41, the card of Dallas Cowboy quarterback Don Meredith. His card accounts for more than 10 percent of the value of the 1961 Fleer set, which sells for substantially more than its Topps counterpart. Out on the West Coast, the set will cost collectors

about $1,200 to $1,500 in top-grade condition. The Meredith card will fetch at least $150 alone, less if it comes with the whole set.

In his playing days, Meredith was known as a cool customer on the field and a wild and reckless soul off the field. He later gained additional fame as a sportscaster on *Monday Night Football* with Frank Gifford and Howard Cosell.

The true Don Meredith is probably best captured by former teammate Peter Gent in his book *North Dallas Forty*, a classic novel of professional football. Gent's character Seth Maxwell is based on the personality of Meredith. Meredith's rookie football card in the 1961 Fleer set is a genuine treasure.

The layout and design of the 1961 Fleer set is solid but has one drawback. The backs are printed in lime green ink that might have been all right when the cards first appeared. After 30 years, however, it has faded badly. In the handful of 1961 Fleer cards I own, it is difficult to see any color at all. The card fronts are good—posed action shots taken in an outdoor setting. The outdoor photography showing sky and clouds enhances the nostalgic quality of the 1961 Fleer cards considerably.

The 1961 Fleer set is superior to the 1961 Topps set in nearly every way—selection, quality, numbers, and design.

In 1962 Topps dug deep into its bag of tricks to upstage Fleer and was successful. The 1962 Topps set contains NFL players only and totals 176 cards. Apparently Topps lost or wouldn't pay for the AFL license in 1962. What Topps lacked in selection

The 1962 Topps set is the first of the famous "black border" designs. *Pictured:* 1962 Topps Jimmy Patton #112.

it made up for with a truly unique design.

This is the famous "black border" set, a design concept that Topps has sprung on football card collectors twice in the history of the hobby. The most recent time was 1985, and the product was worse the second time around. Whenever the chips are down, Topps likes to "run for the borders."

Unfortunately, the black borders mean that it's next to impossible to put together a near-mint set of the 1962 cards. Part of the black border always seems to be missing because of the careless way Topps cut the card sheets in those days. Further aggravating the border problem is the short print problem. Many cards in the 1962 set were printed in smaller numbers than the rest. For collectors it's a tough scramble to find short-printed cards, especially ones that are decently centered.

The 1962 Topps set was oriented horizontally with a posed color photo on the front and a smaller black-and-white insert "action" photo. On many of the cards, the action photo has nothing to do with the player whose name is on the card. It was a good try and would have worked fine if Topps had paid more attention to detail.

One boast this set can make is that it has the first football cards of several authentic stars, including Mike Ditka, Fran Tarkenton, Roman Gabriel, and Billy Kilmer.

Fleer had its own problems in 1962. The third Fleer football set was greatly reduced in number compared to 1961. It pictures AFL players only and numbers 88 cards. Again Fleer chose to show the players in an outdoor setting, in uniform, at practice or in pregame warm-ups.

The card backs are printed in blue and black ink on white stock. Primary colors worked best on early card backs.

But the 1962 Fleer set is only marginally sought by card collectors.

The entire set can be had for less than $600, and it has only two rookie cards of import, those for Fred "The Hammer" Williamson and Ernie Ladd.

Ernie Ladd was the defensive player all coaches dream about, a 6'9" 300-pound giant who usually disdained finesse because his straight-ahead charge was so effective. On pass plays Ladd was capable of literally pounding offensive linemen into the ground, although he was also agile enough to leap over players who tried to cut block him. Ladd's card is not the most expensive in the 1962 Fleer set (Kemp's card is, at $110), but it is the most interesting in a historical sense.

Many people say today that players can't attain Ladd's dimensions

Fleer chose to show players in an outdoor setting in 1962. *Pictured:* 1962 Fleer Jim Norton #52.

without steroids, protein products, vitamins, special diets, and weight training. Ernie Ladd is proof positive that all you really need are the genes of a Goliath.

In 1963 Topps produced 170 NFL cards grouped by teams. The card backs are printed in a weird light orange ink. Mercifully, there is no scratch-off quiz, although the card backs do have a trivia question. This time the answer can be glimpsed by putting red tissue paper over the answer. It's a welcome change.

The card fronts are standard Topps photos—football players without helmets trying to look relaxed for the camera. Some manage the trick; others don't. Football card collectors have decided over the years that they prefer action shots on the card fronts and portraits on the card backs. It took Topps forever to figure out this simple formula.

At about $1,000, the 1963 Topps set is not very high-priced, having only defensive players among the key rookie cards, including Ray Nitschke, Bob Lilly, and Deacon Jones.

Fleer's 89-card 1963 set is smaller but better. All the players come from the AFL and the entire set is, as card dealer Dennis Hooker says, something of a rarity. A key rookie card among the 1963 Fleer cards is that of Len Dawson, a future Super Bowl winner with the Kansas City Chiefs. Another important rookie in this set is #72, Lance Alworth, a speedy receiver who played for the San Diego Chargers.

This hard-to-find 1963 Fleer football set sells for about $1,500 on the hobby market today. The most valuable card is the unnumbered check-list, at $350.

The card backs have brief player biographies and are printed in red and black. More than anything, though, the Fleer 1963 set has a nos-talgic feel that the 1963 Topps set doesn't have. The outdoor setting of the photos and the fact that it's the last issue for an innovative card com-pany contribute to the effect. The following year a new company, Philadelphia Gum, would get into the market, dislodging Topps on the NFL side. Another shakeup was coming to the football card scene, and for a long time afterward, Fleer would be just a minor player.

In the early 1960s, football card design improved overall as a result of the competition between Topps and Fleer. Fleer contributed four su-perior football card sets, and its entry into the market also stimulated dom-inant player Topps to improve the quality of its football cards.

Topps' major design experiments, such as using black borders, printing in unusual colors like orange on the card backs, and eliminating gim-micks like the scratch-off quiz, en-hanced its product. These advances brought a new and welcome matu-rity to the football card scene and a new dignity to a market believed to be, in the 1960s, strictly for kids.

CHAPTER SEVEN

LATE '60s FOOTBALL CARDS

Joe Namath and More

During the mid-1960s, football cards became more closely associated with the glamour of the professional game. At the same time, a startling development occurred in 1964 when Topps was pushed aside by a competitor, the Philadelphia Gum Company. Philly Gum produced its first set of NFL cards in the fall of 1964. Philly Gum outbid Topps for the NFL license, and, having nowhere else to go, Topps outbid Fleer for the AFL license. This effectively shut Fleer out of the major football card market for the next 26 years.

Topps found itself suddenly relegated to second string. For the next four years, Topps made do with AFL cards while Philly Gum ran off a series of four annual NFL sets.

For Topps, it turned out to be a blessing in disguise.

At the same time, a virtual revolution was taking place in the way spectators viewed the game. The revolution was brought about by a videotape recording technique called "instant replay."

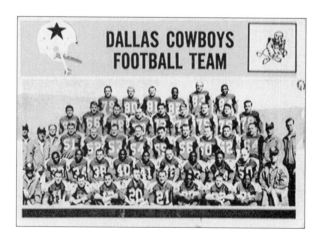

Topps was pushed aside in 1964 by a competitor, the Philadelphia Gum Company. *Pictured:* 1964 Philadelphia Gum Dallas Cowboys #55.

Instant replay was the brainchild of a CBS technician named Tony Verna. Verna first tried out the technique at an Army-Navy game in 1963, showing a long touchdown play a second time as a treat for viewers.

The effect was electric. It was almost as if the public had been waiting all along for this marvel before fully embracing pro football. The instant replay technique spread rapidly across the networks, giving a new allure to all things connected with football, including football cards.

Nevertheless, the 1964 Topps AFL set is a ho-hum affair, consisting of 176 cards, many of which are short printed. There's a cartoon trivia question on the card backs (thankfully not a scratch-off), and the set admittedly contains a few quality rookies. A couple that stand out are San Diego Charger quarterback John Hadl and Oakland Raider quarterback Daryle Lamonica.

But the complete 1964 Topps set is not by any means outstanding. Its only significance is that it serves as a prelude to the outstanding Topps

Only AFL cards were made by Topps in 1964. *Pictured:* 1964 Topps Arch Matsos #144 and 1965 Topps Dee Mackey #120.

49

1965 AFL set, which is the most important football set of the 1960s and is truly one of the great sets of all time.

Two things lift the 1965 Topps set above the rest: First, there's the size of the cards. The ticket-sized cards are a one-time-only phenomenon for Topps; every other Topps set has been cut standard card size. But even more important, the 1965 Topps set is outstanding for a reason that can be summed up in three little words: Joe Willie Namath.

Namath is probably the most idolized football player who ever lived. A big, strong-armed quarterback with an incredibly quick release, he is football's equivalent of Joe DiMaggio. Namath came to symbolize the game at a time when people were beginning to take notice of professional football. Besides, Namath *was* the 1960s. He had long hair, a mustache. He was a rebel. Namath was cool.

It says something when a man titles his autobiography: *I Can't Wait for Tomorrow...Because I Get Better Looking Every Day!* Namath's card, #122 in the 1965 set, sells for about $1,300, fully one-third of the value of the set.

Namath came into professional football from the University of Alabama, where he had been coached by the legendary Paul "Bear" Bryant. His signing was a major coup for the American Football League, then locked in a struggle with the NFL for top-quality collegiate talent. In 1965 Namath was the latest and the best. He signed a $400,000 no-cut contract with Jet owner Sonny Werblin, the biggest ever for a rookie player.

Let's turn back the clock to get a worm's-eye view of the Namath aura. In my high school, you could always tell it was football season because the quarterback of our team, Charlie Clark, would be hobbling around in a cast of some sort. In the spring, when Charlie had healed up, a group of us boys often met to play pickup tackle football at a nearby grade school.

Charlie always wore the same sleeveless sweatshirt. It was of his own design. On the back was a number 12 he'd hand-colored in green marker. Above the number was the name of Namath. As far as Charlie Clark was concerned, Namath was king.

Now, more than 20 years later, the kind of adulation Namath inspired in Charlie Clark continues to inflate the value of this short-printed rookie football card from the 1965 Topps set. It will always be among the top ten cards in the hobby.

The Namath card isn't the only jewel in the 1965 Topps AFL set. Other major rookie cards in this 176-card set include Ben Davidson, Fred Biletnikoff, and cornerback Willie Brown, all of the Raiders.

Brown's card in particular is undervalued. During his years with the Raiders, Brown was a bump and run specialist without peer. He often shut out opposing receivers and was a one-man nightmare for quarterbacks who tended to let their passes float. Brown's card in near-mint goes for about $12.

Willie Brown was recognized by his peers when he was enshrined in the Pro Football Hall of Fame in 1984. After the landmark 1965 set,

The card fronts of the 1966 Topps set were bordered by a ridiculous TV screen layout. *Pictured:* 1966 Topps Sherrill Headrick #69.

Topps football cards went rapidly downhill. The 1966 set was bordered by one of those ridiculous TV-screen layouts so beloved by the Brooklyn gum company. In a word, it's horrible.

Topps did a little better in 1967, inventing a nice portrait effect on the card fronts by placing the team names over the shoulders of the players pictured.

The four Philly Gum sets issued between 1964 and 1967 have some good cards and features as well.

The 198-card 1964 Philadelphia Gum NFL set is an above average set of football cards. It doesn't soar on silken wings, but then again it doesn't exactly sink to the bottom. Major rookies in the set are Merlin Olsen and Jack Pardee. No big-time quarterbacks. No running backs. If it weren't somewhat rare and hard to find on the hobby market, it might not cost the $700 it fetches in top-grade condition.

Key elements in the 1964 Philly design are the blue and black ink used on the backs and the extremely simple front layout. The idea of using an occasional action shot does not appear to have occurred to football card company photographers in those years. Philly and Topps just had players stand on the sidelines in team uniform mugging for the camera.

In recent years card makers have gotten around the problem of the helmet obscuring the player's face by putting a smaller portrait photo on the card back. That gives them the entire front to show a player the way we want to see him—in action. It is the obvious and ideal solution.

Philly Gum actually thought to include a player photo on each of its card backs in 1966, but the photo was part of a quiz rather than a portrait of the player the card featured. Too bad.

In 1965 Philly Gum produced another above average set, although it can't compare with its Topps coun-

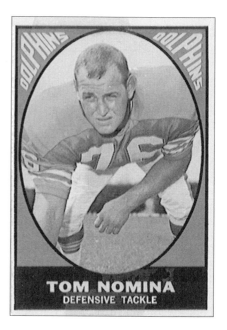

Topps did a little better in 1967 with a nice portrait effect. *Pictured, from left to right:* 1967 Topps Sid Blanks #51 and 1967 Topps Tom Nomina #86.

terpart. Philly used almost exactly the same style on its second NFL set, another 198-card entry, as it did on the first. The player pictures lack distinction, although they are all sharply focused and close up.

Two defensive stars, Mel Renfro and Carl Eller, in addition to one receiver, Paul Warfield, are the key rookies in the 1965 Philly Gum set. It goes for about $500 in near-mint condition.

Philadelphia Gum grew a bit bolder in 1966, coming out with what proved to be its most memorable set. Included in the 1966 set is the aforementioned quiz game. The company switched the player name from the bottom front of the cards to the top front, which helps the set enormously. The change seems to open up the cards a bit, providing more space for the photo. On the backs, the player information is brief and to the point. The quiz is harmless enough since the answers are on other cards. There's none of that scratch-off business to ruin the card.

The extra-special thing about the 1966 set is the rookie card of Gale Sayers, Chicago Bear legend and author of an uplifting biography, *I Am Third*. Known for his personal charisma as well as for the extraordinary friendship he had with teammate and cancer victim Brian Piccolo, Sayers is an example of the best of what pro football is all about. The story of his friendship with Piccolo was the subject of a TV-movie made in 1970, with Billy Dee Williams as Sayers and James Caan as Piccolo. The film was called *Brian's Song*.

To be sure, pro football is a game

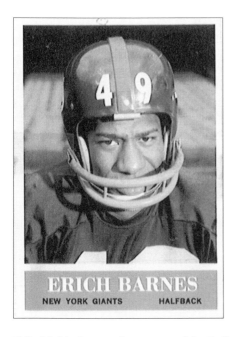

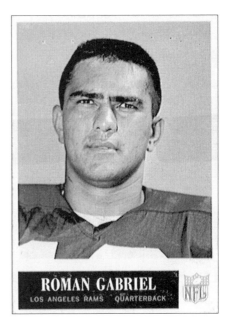

Philadelphia Gum made many good football cards from 1964 to 1967. *Pictured, from left to right:* 1964 Philadelphia Gum Erich Barnes #113 and 1965 Philadelphia Gum Roman Gabriel #87.

and a business, but lessons in the ways of men are there to be learned for those willing to probe under the surface. In the ultra-masculine occupation of football, there is probably no finer example of a man with courage and the capacity for personal growth than Gale Sayers.

The Sayers NFL rookie card is #38 in the Philadelphia Gum set. It will cost a collector anywhere from $200 to $500. Even at the higher figure, it is well worth it.

Brian Piccolo's only card is #26 in the 1969 Topps NFL set. At $75 to $100, the Piccolo card is moderately priced, though rising fast.

Another Chicago Bear of considerable fame, Dick Butkus, graces the 1966 Philly Gum set. No one who has ever seen game film of Butkus at

work can deny he is one of the great linebackers in NFL history. Woe unto him who got in Butkus's way!

The Butkus card, #31 in the 1966 set, goes for about half the price of the Sayers card. It is also well worth owning if you get tired of cards of conventional offensive stars.

The last set for Philadelphia Gum came in 1967. Like the others, this final set was complete at 198 cards. It does not contain any individual player cards that collectors are much interested in, but it has value as a record of the league that year. If the 1964 and 1965 Philly Gum sets can be considered above average and the 1966 set well above average, the 1967 set is below average.

The simple truth is that the Philly Gum NFL cards of the 1960s are all overshadowed by the inclusion of the AFL Namath rookie card in the 1965 Topps set. The later Topps issues are overshadowed as well.

For collectors, the main thing to know about sets of the 1960s is which one contains the Namath rookie. Though all the rest may contain cards of interest and value, they are mere pretenders compared to the Topps 1965 offering.

The reason is that football is food for the imagination as well as for the spirit. No one captures the imagination of the fans better than the guy who had it all, Joe Willie Namath.

CHAPTER EIGHT

TOPPS' 20-YEAR MONOPOLY

The Only Football Cards, 1968–1988

The longest single monopoly in the history of football cards was Topps' from 1968 to 1988. After 1988 the football card scene once again changed and put us in the present period, a time of unbelievably varied choices.

Many card collectors have strong feelings of antipathy toward Topps. That's because the football card releases the company put out during the years it had the market all to itself were often dismal.

In truth, the Topps efforts in the years 1968–1989 are characterized by card issues that are not just dull but in some cases downright ugly. Starting with the 1968 set, Topps made annual card sets that went beyond mere mediocrity; they have an uncanny ability to repel collectors.

The 1968 Topps set is the first combined AFL/NFL set since 1961. Although the league didn't formally merge until 1970, interleague games were becoming commonplace. Fans no longer had to speculate about which league had the better teams. Now they knew.

The 219-card 1968 Topps set is a good example of great player selec-tion hobbled by a tired design. Again Topps resurrected the "coin rub" scratch-off games on the card backs, a feature so destructive to earlier sets. Another bad idea was issuing the cards in two separate series. The later series was guaranteed to be scarcer because interest in football cards usu-ally wanes as the season goes on. For some reason this is less of a factor now than it was in the late 1960s.

The main reason that the Topps 1968 design ultimately does not work is that it's dull. Anybody with a smidgen of artistic talent could do the same or better. Player names are enclosed in a little blob at the bottom of the card, and the team logo occu-pies the upper left corner. The pho-tography is poor because nearly all the pictures are posed awkwardly.

It's particularly sad that the 1968 set is so lousy because it boasts some standout rookie quarterbacks—Bob Griese, Jim Hart, and Craig Mor-ton—as well as running back Floyd Little.

To compound the insult, Topps used the 1968 set as a model for the two that follow, the 1969 and 1970 sets.

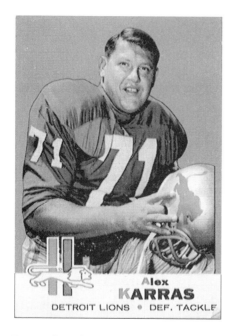

Topps released many poor football sets after gaining a monopoly in 1968. O. J. Simpson's rookie card is about all that holds up a really dismal 1970 set. *Pictured, from left to right:* 1969 Topps Alex Karras #123 and 1970 Topps O. J. Simpson #90.

Card production in 1969 and 1970 increased to 263 items per set, but inspiration is absent from these efforts too. You can get a good idea of how little the hobby regards these sets by looking at the combined near-mint value of all three—barely $1,500. The only thing holding up the value of the very poor 1970 set is the rookie card of O. J. Simpson, priced at about $200. To date, Simpson's bizarre and well-publicized murder case has had little effect on the value of his cards. Apparently most football card collectors are not so ghoulish as to get into a bidding war for Simpson memorabilia.

The biggest problem in the 1969 set is that half the cards were printed without borders. Finding borderless 1969 Topps football cards in near-mint is extremely difficult.

Borderless cards look great in the beginning. But no matter how careful you are, the edges eventually become frayed.

Another card typifying the low quality of Topps football cards in the period is the 1970 card of Bob Griese—#10 in the set and Griese's second mainstream football card. This fine Miami quarterback is shown holding the ball cocked back in a pose so patently artificial you have to laugh. Griese deserves better.

In 1971 things began to improve a little. In the 263-card 1971 set, Topps came up with a distinctive design for the first time in years. The blue and red borders on the card fronts have the solid eye appeal of primary colors. On the backs, the text is printed in black with gold accents on the gray card stock. No scratch-offs or games mar this set; the cards contain just straight information and stats. The Topps 1971 set is what football cards from that period should have looked like all along.

In 1972 Topps made a commendable decision to greatly expand card production for football. The 1972 set leaps to a total of 351 cards. The production increase coincides with the burgeoning popularity of the game nationally.

Professional football, long in the shadow of the hugely popular sport of baseball, was finally coming into its own. Across the country on Sunday afternoons, stadiums were filling with swarms of screaming fans. Thanks to the proliferation of tele-vised games, professional football stars, once known only to fans in a few Eastern cities, were now household names.

In 1973 Topps increased football card production again, this time raising the number of cards in the annual set to 528. This was the first "megaset" to hit the football card hobby. A megaset is a set that pictures more than one-third of the players in the league. Many of the football card sets produced after the Topps monopoly ended in 1989 are also megasets.

The design and layout of the Topps football cards produced from 1973 through 1982 are not particularly significant. Virtually all of the sets after the 1971 gem feature cheap, poorly conceived design. It is as if the

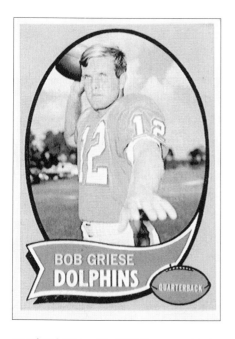
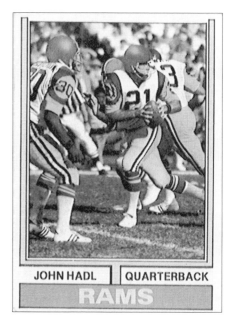

Another low-quality 1970 Topps card belongs to Bob Griese. Almost no 1970s quarterback had a decent card. *Pictured, from left to right:* **1970 Topps Bob Griese #10 and 1974 Topps John Hadl #50.**

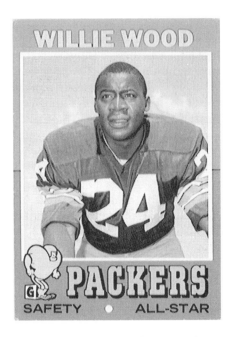

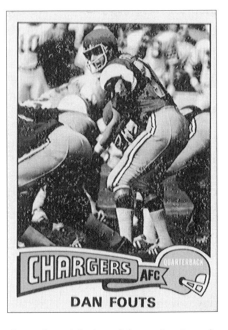

In 1971 Topps managed a distinctive design. *Pictured:* 1971 Topps Willie Wood #55.

The style and design of the cards released by Topps from 1973 to 1982 are undistinguished. *Pictured:* 1975 Topps Dan Fouts #367.

company could not be bothered to put much thought into its football cards. Over in the baseball card hobby, by contrast, the cards made by Topps were consistently upgraded, and there are many superb annual issues scattered in these years.

Every year from 1973 to 1982, Topps gave the hobby a fairly inclusive set of players. But the frills that make collectors happy are nearly all missing. In fairness to Topps, the company probably never had any notion that its designs would be examined in detail by rabid collectors. Topps simply made football cards, lots of them. Quantity was there, but quality was not.

A good example of the low-qual-ity product Topps put out in this period is the 1981 set, featuring the Joe Montana rookie card, #216. This first card appearance of the man who might be the best quarterback in the history of football is just terrible. It's so bad that the San Francisco emblem has been crudely airbrushed from Joe's helmet. No doubt Topps got a price break on the license by not using copyrighted NFL logos. Montana's first card is a piece of history now valued at $150 to $200. The Montana card would be significantly higher in price if it were a better quality card.

Art Monk's card has a value approaching $100. But thanks to Topps' cheapness and lack of interest, the rest of the cards are of no consequence to collectors. This fairly old set sells for only about $300 in near-mint.

In 1983 Topps cut production to 396 cards. Like all the sets produced by Topps in the 1980s, these sets are interesting only to the most dedicated collectors. However much you may love football and enjoy card collecting, this is not a good product. In spite of the rapid advances in printing techniques and computer graphics, Topps was putting out the same old stuff. The card stock is low-grade, the photos are poor, and in 1983 the rookie selection was pathetic. There were some great rookies in the league that year, but none appeared on the Topps cards.

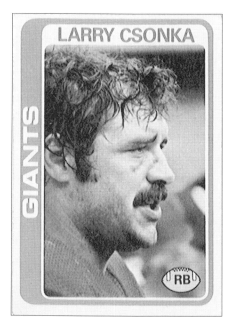

Even though Topps' card designs of the '70s left much to be desired, each year the company gave the hobby a fairly inclusive set of players. *Pictured:* 1978 Topps Larry Csonka #25.

On the other hand, 1983 did mark the first appearance of a few fine players, including Marcus Allen, Mike Singletary, and Jim McMahon. But even these bright lights aren't enough to bring a shine to a card set collectors consider dull, dull, dull. Paying any more than $75 for the entire set in top condition is a royal waste of money.

In 1984 the Topps USFL set produced more interesting football cards than the NFL set. The USFL set is clearly better for selection, quality, and scarcity. (See Chapter 13 for a full examination of the Topps USFL sets.)

The 1984 Topps NFL set again has 396 cards. There are more than a handful of authentic stars in this set, although the design is the usual ho-hum affair. Names that appear here for the first time include John Elway, Eric Dickerson, and Dan Marino. The set is notable for Team Leader cards and a Topps 1984 one-time-only feature, the Instant Replay card.

An Instant Replay card came after the regular card for a number of players in the 1984 set. The Instant Replay cards focused on special players credited with a standout season the previous year and on those who had enjoyed long-term careers. Instant Replay cards exist for nearly all the top names in the NFL that year.

The 1984 Topps set is plagued by more than the average number of errors, omissions, and mistakes. Card #9, the Super Bowl card, has the score from the 1983 Super Bowl listed incorrectly. Perhaps the proofreading on the 1984 set was done by a person who prefers tennis.

In 1985 Topps decided to get out of its rut and released an absolutely weird 396-card set. It is one of two funereal "black border" Topps sets. The first was issued in 1962. Not only are the cards edged in black (as if somebody had died), but the cards are also oriented horizontally. You have to turn the card on its side to look at the photo, a big drawback in album display.

The 1985 set is proof that whenever the staff at Topps is fresh out of ideas, they can go into the archives and dig out a chestnut to foist on card collectors. The most sought-after card in the 1985 set belongs to quarterback Warren Moon, who came to the NFL after a stellar career in Canada.

Moon is known around the league as the quarterback who throws the prettiest, straightest passes in the game. Even Moon's rare interceptions are widely admired for their tight spirals. But while Moon's passes might be pretty, his first NFL football card is not. Moon's card, #251 in the set, has the same miserable design as the rest, pushing the card value below $40.

The last three sets of the Topps monopoly—1986, 1987, and 1988—must be grouped together because they are so similar in style.

Like the preceding sets, they contain 396 cards each. The most valuable of these three sets is the 1986 set, which sells in near-mint for about $100.

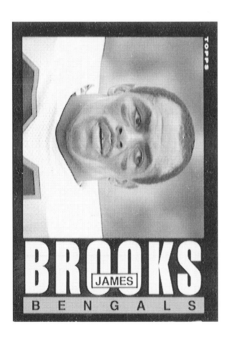

The 1985 Topps set is the second "black border" set produced by the company. *Pictured:* 1985 Topps James Brooks #213.

Red Grange, "The Galloping Ghost," suffered a knee injury that eventually ended his career. *Pictured:* 1991 Pro Set Red Grange #77.

There are many famous players with first cards in these three sets, including Bernie Kosar, Boomer Esiason, Randall Cunningham, Jim Everett, Cornelius Bennett, and Chris Miller. Otherwise there isn't much positive to say about these cards. When collectors sort through these cards at a show or in a dealer's shop, it's a bit difficult to tell them apart. The players deserve better than this.

The dismal set Topps issued in 1988, the last year it owned the NFL football card market, shows how completely Topps underestimated the market.

You might think Topps had grown tired of making football cards, given the poor quality of the stuff it dumped on collectors. The 1988 set is the usual Topps product printed on natural stock with boring photos on the card fronts. There's some gimmick in the set about "Super Rookies" and also some attention paid to All-Pro players. Bo Jackson's first regular football card appears in this set as well.

Jackson's case is sad and a clear reminder of the fleeting quality of success in sports. In a way he is like Red Grange, the "Galloping Ghost," who eventually suffered a knee injury that limited his running ability.

"I was never the same player after that," Grange said later.

Bo Jackson's hip injury came in a game against the Cincinnati Bengals. On TV millions watched the tackle that ended Jackson's career. Bo's rookie card, #327 in the 1988 Topps set, was once selling for as much as $20. It is now a 10-cent common.

Without Jackson the 1988 Topps set is nothing. And if you were a collector in 1988, Topps was your only choice in football cards. It was either Topps or forget it. The company motto could easily have been: "At Topps we don't have to try very hard."

If you look at the 1986, 1987, and 1988 Topps sets, you can see why the Topps monopoly finally had to end. For a full generation, Topps seemed content to distribute a second-rate product. As the only national supplier of football cards, Topps could take full advantage of the opportunity to swell profits at the expense of quality.

If ever there was a textbook example of how a monopoly works to the detriment of customers, Topps football card production from the late 1960s through the 1980s is it. Football fans and card collectors alike should remember the Topps monopoly when they are tempted to complain about the glut of football cards now filling the shelves. It could be worse. We could be back in the 1970s and 1980s, when Topps was the only football card game in town.

A similar monopoly has long existed on the field, where fans of the professional game have had only one league to follow. Only diehard NFL fans would dispute the contention that the NFL game played today can be rigid and almost unbearably predictable. Although innovators like Darrell "Mouse" Davis can promote the run-and-shoot offense in the CFL and elsewhere, not even the Houston Oilers have gone full bore with it in the NFL.

Since 1991 a new league called the Professional Spring Football

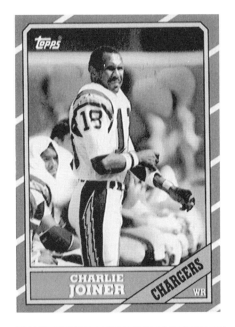

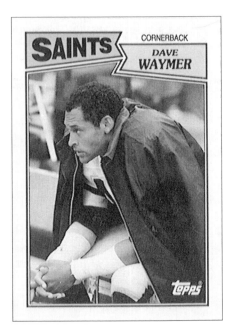

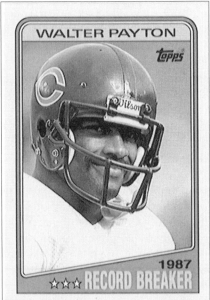

The last three Topps sets make it evident why the monopoly ended. *Pictured, clockwise from top left:* 1986 Topps Charlie Joiner #236, 1987 Topps Dave Waymer #280, and 1988 Topps Walter Payton #5.

League, or PSFL, has been in the making. Still another fledgling pro league, the North American Football League, has been talked up in sports circles, both in Canada and in the United States. Either league would give hundreds of mid-range players jobs in the sport and raise a few to stardom.

Another league is the Arena Football League, which features a seven-man 50-yard indoor version of the sport. Arena teams now employ about 300 players.

As we can see by looking at Topps football cards from 1968 to 1988, a monopoly is not in the best interest of players, sports fans, or collectors. Here's hoping the PSFL, the NAFL, Arena Football, and a newly aggressive CFL are more than just thorns in the side of the big league.

CHAPTER NINE

THE REVOLUTION OF 1989

When Football Cards Broke Free

In 1989, with little fanfare, a revolution took place in the football card hobby. There was an explosion of interest in trading cards of all types, but the football card hobby in particular underwent rapid expansion.

It's ironic because for years football card collecting was a hobby backwater, eliciting little praise and less interest. You can get a fascinating insight into the growth of the hobby by checking out the *Sport Americana Football, Hockey, Basketball, and Boxing Card Price Guide* from the year 1981 and comparing the prices listed there to today's prices.

A comparison shows that the past 13 years have been a time of unprecedented growth in the football card hobby. Football card prices in 1981 averaged about 10 percent of current prices. Old-line material was unbelievably cheap as the decade opened. The 1935 National Chicle set was priced in the 1981 *Sport Americana* at less than $1,000. The Nagurski card had a tag of $125 in mint. Beginning in the year 1981 and accelerating after 1989, the football card hobby has undergone what can only be called a revolution. Its effects

may be summed up as follows: More and better cards for everybody.

Topps Chewing Gum company had monopolized the football card market for an entire generation, 1968 to 1988. In 1989 that changed. Spurred by the 1981 end of the Topps monopoly in the baseball card hobby, the Topps football card monopoly crashed spectacularly. In essence the owners and players in the NFL decided they'd make more money if they let other companies have a crack at making football cards.

They were right. They did make more money—lots of it. Topps had used its exclusive arrangement to get rich for years. In Topps' favor, it must be said that the company kept prices low for cards, targeting the small-fry market. But Topps sold an inferior product to kids who had no other place to go. By 1986 the football cards Topps released were no longer even industry standard, let alone cutting edge.

In 1989 Topps released a set totaling 396 cards. It's one of Topps' usual sets, printed with green and yellow ink on the natural cardboard backs. The front photos are largely sideline shots of players with their helmets off. Very few are action photos, the kind collectors have come to expect in newer sets. The only fresh design feature on these cards is the colored stripes on the upper part of the card fronts.

There's little to say about the Topps set. These are old-fashioned football cards with few arresting features and cannot be recommended under most circumstances. Collectors have not shown much interest in the set, and today a full factory set of the 1989 Topps cards sells for $15 or so. This set isn't quite worthless, but it's close to it.

In 1989 the Topps set looked especially bad because that year not one but three hot new companies is-

sued card sets—Pro Set, Score, and Action Packed. Pro Set got started in the football card business by way of publishing Game Day programs for the NFL. The 1989 set was its first.

Pro Set's 440-card NFL set is highly attractive, especially when compared to the 1989 Topps set. There was some controversy over card #47A, the infamous William Perry error card. A host of collectors decided all at once that they must have the Perry card at any cost.

The Perry card was an error card because Pro Set released it before they had "The Refrigerator" signed to a card deal. Pro Set had to recall the card, but not before many of the cards had already slipped out.

Pro Set soon substituted rookie Ron Morris for Perry as card #47B, and a storm of bidding for #47A quickly ensued. At the height of the frenzy in the spring of 1990, price guides like *Dellafera's Football Card Monthly* had it listed for $100.

Buying the Perry card at $100 was an expensive lesson for many newcomers to the hobby. What goes up can also come down. An error card is, after all, a mistake. Printing errors are much more common than coinage errors because the mint obviously has more at stake than chewing gum and card companies.

In the spring of 1990, a lot of collectors bought Pro Set's elusive William "Refrigerator" Perry error card only to see its value disintegrate in the months following purchase. After peaking at $100, the Perry card plunged fast. Within two years it was selling in the hobby magazines as a $5 special.

Later Perry did sign a deal with

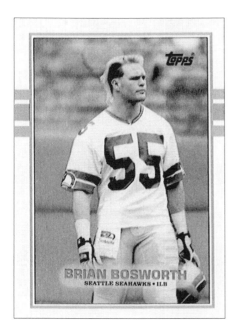

The colored stripes on the card fronts are one fresh design feature on the 1989 Topps set. *Pictured:* 1989 Topps Brian Bosworth #192.

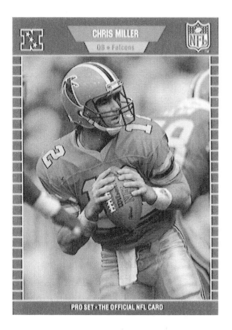

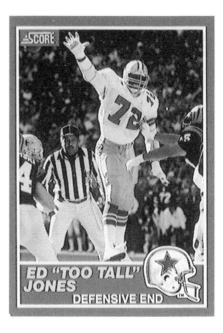

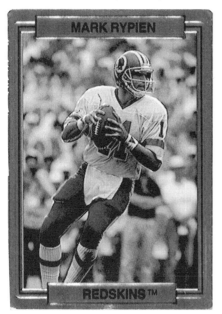

In 1989 three hot new companies issued card sets—Pro Set, Score, and Action Packed. *Pictured, clockwise from top left:* 1989 Pro Set Chris Miller #12, 1989 Score Ed "Too Tall" Jones #5, and 1989 Action Packed Mark Rypien #29.

Pro Set, and the 1989 Pro Set non-error Perry card eventually appeared as #445 in the Pro Set high number Series II cards.

Today the Perry #47A card is still a novelty, but it's a novelty something like fool's gold.

Otherwise the 1989 Pro Set effort

is a solid achievement—nothing spectacular, nothing truly rare, just a lot of good cards for collectors to own, admire, and maybe invest in. The design is colorful, and the player selection is top-notch. It will probably never be very valuable because Pro Set has always printed more NFL cards than the market could bear.

Kmart and Walgreen's stores load shelves with Pro Set cards for sale around the holidays. Because of the glut, the 1989 set still hovers around $20, although collectors can probably get a hand-collated set from a dealer for about $12.

The most successful of the four major sets from 1989 is the 330-card Score factory set. In every manner, shape, and form, this is the top NFL football card set to emerge from the 1980s. Collectors agree that there are none to compare with it as far as selection, quality, design, rookies, and scarcity are concerned. This is it.

A brief glance at the set reveals a few of the treasures this near-perfect grouping has to offer:

Michael Irvin rookie—card #18. This Dallas receiver has done everything asked of him—and more. The Cowboys have reason to believe that they may be the team of the 1990s, just as the San Francisco 49ers were the team of the 1980s. Flashy, talented receivers like Irvin will help keep them on top.

Chris Miller rookie—card #60. The Glanville-coached Falcons

Pro Set's 1989 NFL set is highly attractive. *Pictured:* 1989 Pro Set Frank Minnifield #82 front and reverse.

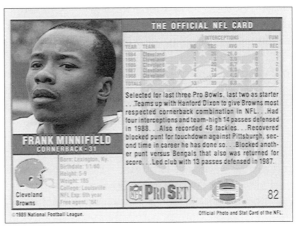

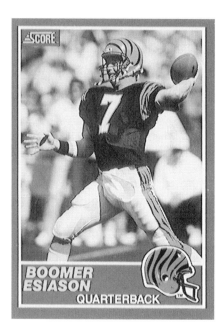

The most successful 1989 set is the 330-card offering by Score. *Pictured:* 1989 Score Boomer Esiason #3.

weren't everybody's cup of Gatorade, but even Falcon faultfinders had to admit Miller was a tough and heady competitor.

Mark Rypien rookie—card #105. Would Washington have made it to Super Bowl XXVI without Rypien? The answer is no.

Thurman Thomas rookie—card #211. Yes, it's true. This set has everybody. Thomas is the soul and spirit of the Buffalo Bills. By any measure the Thomas card is a winner.

Barry Sanders rookie—card #257. The Detroit Lions are a star-crossed team with a glorious history and a great tradition. Though it's unlikely they'll make the Super Bowl in his career (barring a coaching change), Barry Sanders is and always

will be a part of the Detroit Lion story.

Troy Aikman rookie—card #270. Can the 1989 Score football set get any better? The Dallas quarterback is the prototype "golden boy" star of this powerful Cowboy team.

Many other rookie names in the 1989 Score set deserve mention— Andre Rison, Dieon Sanders, Eric Metcalf, Steve Atwater, and more. The many action photos alone put the set way beyond Topps 1989. *Tuff Stuff's* price guide goes so far as to call the Score 1989 football set the "Rolls Royce" of recent sets. It is right on the button in saying so.

The Score 1989 set, as we have seen, has much to recommend it. It is a great set and a major change from the very tepid Topps fare from the same year. However, nice as it is, the design is not quite revolutionary. That laurel belongs to another, much smaller set, the 30-card Action Packed 1989 test set.

The 1989 Action Packed test set is one of those rare football card sets to break new design ground. Before 1989 card makers had never produced anything quite like Action Packed's "sculpted" cards. On the card fronts, the player picture is raised to follow the body outline, so the photo has a "feel" as well as a look. Because this is the first appearance of an important new feature, the 1989 Action Packed test set might eventually be considered one of the all-time great football sets.

The sculpted AP cards are in a class with the 1952 Bowman large set and the 1935 National Chicle. The Action Packed cards encouraged competitors to try new design experiments and touched off a virtual firestorm of innovation and competition.

As a bonus, the 1989 Action Packed test set also includes a rookie card for Super Bowl XXVI hero Mark Rypien. Common as multiple rookie cards are now, they were a relative rarity as recently as 1989. Some fans liked throwing rocks at Rypien when the Washington team had an off year, as it did in 1992. But smart football card collectors will say "So what?" and go right on building up a portfolio of Rypien cards.

Why? Because Rypien took his team to the Super Bowl and won it. Given a chance, he could do it somewhere else again.

The annual Dallas-Washington slugfests are mean-spirited affairs that thrill NFL fans. Television ratings underscore this assertion in a big way.

When Dallas and Washington are both contending for the NFC East title, their games invariably wind up on national TV. In the past, Nielsen ratings have jumped as much as 22 percent for Dallas-Washington contests. Though the players may change as the teams evolve, there is something about this relatively new rivalry that always gets the fans pumped.

The 1989 Action Packed test set divides into three teams, the most prominent of which is Washington. The other two are the Chicago Bears and the Giants. High-interest players featured in the set include Lawrence Taylor, Joe Morris, Neal Anderson, Kelvin Bryant, Phil Simms, Mark Bavaro, Dave Meggett, Art Monk, Trace Armstrong, and Wilber Marshall.

But it's not the players that make this set so memorable. Selection is just a bonus. The set's outstanding feature is the visionary use of advanced printing techniques to produce an entirely new concept, the ultra premium sculpted football card.

Action Packed and collectors in the hobby were so pleased with the 1989 design that no one minded when the company used it again in the more ambitious 281-card 1990 set.

For a full tour de force display of what Action Packed could do with its singular design, the complete 281-card 1990 Action Packed factory set is the place to look. What the 1989 test set promises, the 1990 full set delivers. The 1990 Action Packed fac-

What the 1989 Action Packed test set promises, the full 1990 set delivers. *Pictured:* 1990 Action Packed Steve Largent #254.

tory set is also significant because it includes the unnumbered Jim Plunkett braille card. Player information on AP braille cards may be read by people trained in this read-by-touch aid to the blind.

The 1991 Action Packed set followed up on this good idea with an eight-card braille subset. It's one of many special touches made possible by AP's sculpting technology. At length AP went overboard with a series of embarrassingly deluxe gold cards, but that detracts only a little from its original achievement.

The world of football cards turned upside down in the year 1989. That year led off the best and wildest time ever in the history of our hobby. What followed has been exciting and exasperating, sometimes profitable and sometimes not. But it can always be called fascinating for collectors of football cards.

And it happens to be the time we're in now.

The world of football cards was turned upside down in 1989 by new companies like Score and Pro Set. *Pictured:* 1989 Pro Set Bob Golic #460.

CHAPTER TEN

'90s FOOTBALL CARDS AND BEYOND

Above the High Water Mark

In 1990 five companies fielded major sets of football cards: Action Packed, Fleer, Pro Set, Score, and Topps.

But the real flood hit in 1991, when no less than 15 major nationally distributed NFL sets inundated the market. They included the following: Action Packed, Bowman, Classic, Fleer, Fleer Ultra, Pacific, Pro Set, Pro Set Platinum, Score, Score Pinnacle, Star Pics, Topps, Topps Stadium Club, Upper Deck, and Wild Card. The list is more extensive if you add in a World League set, two Canadian sets, and a host of inserts, specials, and updates.

Some collectors would argue that the 1991 Pro Line set ought to be included as well.

Others disagree. The Pro Line cards are not football cards, they say, but fashion cards of football players and their wives decked out in cool threads. Most people in the hobby have shown little interest in the Pro Line product. The entire 300-card set sells for under $10.

By the summer of 1992, seven new issues had hit the stores. As the summer wore on, new card sets appeared almost weekly until the total reached 22 by year's end.

Card makers had joined the football card "gold rush" begun in 1991 by Action Packed. The seven earliest issues were sets by Pro Set, Pacific, Fleer, SkyBox, Action Packed, Collector's Edge, and Classic. Two of the companies, Collector's Edge and SkyBox, were newcomers to the foot-

Some collectors say 1991 Pro Line cards are nothing more than fashion cards. *Pictured:* 1991 Pro Line Jennifer Montana #SC1.

71

ball card arena, although SkyBox could boast success in 1991 with a highly regarded NBA basketball series.

Football card collectors had to be excused for feeling stupefied by the sheer number of new cards coming on the market. Dealers were also confused. Retail dealer Dave Kelts of

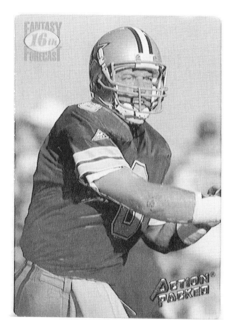

Eugene Sports Cards in Oregon echoed many in the profession when he said that the huge number of releases posed a problem for retailers.

"You can't stock all the football issues anymore. It's overwhelming. And plenty of guesswork goes into what you order from wholesalers. Instead of buying cases, I'm down to buying boxes, hoping to pick out what my customers will go for."

Did football card collectors have any reason to go for the tide of 1992 releases? A brief look at representative sets gives you some idea of what collectors had to consider.

Action Packed moved to claim the ultra high end of the hobby, with 280 regular cards, eight braille cards, and forty-two 24K gold cards. The unique Action Packed sculpted imagery was again featured, along with some minor improvements to the overall design. The 24K cards were part of the company's Mint Collection. These special cards came crafted in gold leaf and fit in a box lined in black velour. Mint Collection cards had a suggested retail price of $200 for a pack of six. Each of the six was pro-

The unique sculpted imagery on Action Packed cards sets them apart. *Pictured, right:* 1994 Action Packed Emmitt Smith WS1; *above:* 1994 Action Packed Troy Aikman FF5.

tected by an individual parchment slipsheet.

What can be said about gold football cards? They seem out of place in the hobby. Maybe they would work for polo. The regular Action Packed set was good, but the mint cards bordered on the ridiculous.

Classic issued a 1992 draft pick set containing 100 cards, expanding the field beyond its 1991 release, which numbered only 50 cards. Making a concession to the high-end mania gripping the hobby, Classic randomly inserted 10 limited edition gold cards.

With the possible exceptions of Desmond Howard and Tommy Maddox, few of the players in the Classic set have Hall of Fame potential. Another drawback of the set is that the players are pictured in college uniforms, making the cards something less than true rookie cards. Collectors wanting ground-floor investments would probably be better off buying select single cards of talented rookies in pro uniform.

Collector's Edge came up with a new idea for its 175-card set: the indestructible football card. The solid plastic stock won't tear or fray and easily handles immersion in water.

Unfortunately, the backs of the 1992 Collector's Edge cards have a substance on them that makes the card cling to any smooth surface. It's annoying to have these cards gum together once the paper covering is removed.

Pro Set 1992 was nearly identical to Pro Set 1991. The only obvious change was a new typeface used on the text. The high-quality camera work continues for collectors who

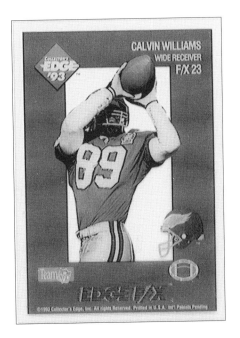

Collector's Edge cards are solid plastic. *Pictured:* 1993 Collector's Edge Calvin Williams #FX 23.

appreciate photographic values. Like Score, Pro Set produced a 700-card megaset, including specials, rookies, and novelty cards.

Once you got past the sizzle to examine the steak, the NFL football cards issued in 1992 had a tiresome sameness. A look at the numbers reveals why: There are about 1,200 active NFL-level pro football players in the United States. Manufacturers issued millions of cards depicting the same players over and over again. In the long run, it had to have a depressing effect on the hobby.

Because of the large numbers, Indianapolis dealer Bob Merrill of Indy's Wholesale Ballcard noted that shelf life for football cards shrank to about three weeks.

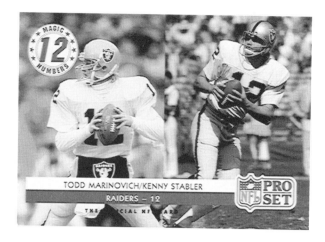

Many 1992 football cards had a tiresome sameness. *Pictured:* **1992 Pro Set Todd Marinovich/Kenny Stabler #350.**

"After that," Merrill says, "interest was mainly from folks trying to fill sets. The exception was PrimeTime. I remember it was late December and sales were still going strong, probably because of PrimeTime's good selection and the Costacos Brothers Poster Cards, which kids seem to like."

The Costacos Brothers Poster Cards were palm-sized versions of giant posters the brothers produced for a gallery of major NFL stars.

The 360-card SkyBox PrimeTime series edged out GameDay among later 1992 cards for quality and selection. PrimeTime included more than five dozen rookie cards, most of which (46 out of 71) feature players in NFL uniform. Many other sets fall down badly on this key point.

If a player is an NFL rookie, do we want to see him in his college togs? Guess again. SkyBox hired photographers to record the rookies in uniform at camp and preseason games. The rookies helped fuel PrimeTime's late success.

The Costacos brothers produced card-sized versions of posters for a gallery of NFL stars. *Pictured:* **Jerry Rice PrimeTime Costacos card.**

Where SkyBox PrimeTime really hit the mark was in the way this set was released to the public. Only 10,000 cases were produced, and they were offered through hobby dealers only. Cases moved fast.

Dealers, not retailers, are the bedrock of the hobby, giving us places where cards may be purchased, traded, and sold. When a local dealer quits, area hobbyists are hurt. SkyBox deserved applause for supporting dealers via PrimeTime.

Bob Merrill saw his SkyBox PrimeTime product sell out. "After I ordered a second batch, they told me that was it for 1992 PrimeTime."

The PrimeTime cards were also decently priced at a suggested retail of $1.75.

SkyBox PrimeTime really hit the mark. *Pictured:* 1992 SkyBox PrimeTime Steve Emtman #S1.

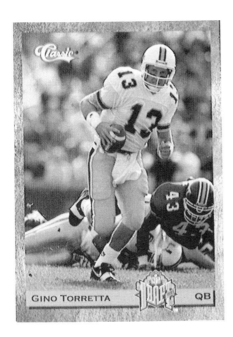

If a player is an NFL rookie, do we want to see him in college togs? *Pictured:* 1993 Classic Gino Torreta #98.

The other big 1992 football card story was unquestionably the NFL GameDay phenomenon. At 500 cards, this was a large set in more ways than one. GameDay skipped the subsets and specials, offering instead a vast player selection with literally dozens of rookies.

The ticket-sized cards are a throwback to the 1965 Topps AFL set, and they captured the fancy of the hobby in 1992. GameDay's slick front design used combination color and monochrome images. Priced at around $1.50 per pack, GameDay was a winner.

Both All World's and Bowman's 1992 football issues were very rare, but collectors became interested in Bowman's while ignoring All World's. The Bowman issue got hot

GameDay's ticket-sized cards are a throwback to the rare Topps 1965 set. *Pictured:* 1993 GameDay Ron Woodson #26.

other draft pick sets in this bunch. The Star Pics cards have a sharper design and higher production values than Courtside, but the two sets are otherwise quite similar. The Courtside cards are marred by numerous poor photos and by Courtside's ultraviolet coating, which reeked of formaldehyde. Allergy sufferers should be wary of the Courtside cards as an environmental hazard.

Incidentally, the appearance of the Star Pics football cards marked the end for that company. It went bankrupt in early 1993, owing its printer a large sum of money.

Last but not least was Wild Card. Critics sniped at Wild Card's 1992 460-card NFL entry because of the

in 1992 because word went out that it was scarce. Long-time collectors familiar with 1992 Bowman cards don't believe that they were quite good enough to justify the $270 price tag seen on the set. But All World's 1992 NFL cards were so rare that some collectors were sure that they did not really exist.

At the bottom of the pile was the Topps regular release. The cards had little to recommend them.

The 113 Star Pics cards and the 140 Courtside cards were the two

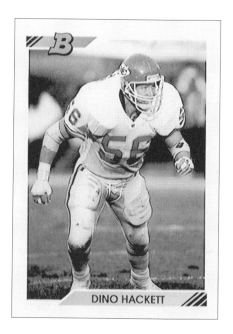

Bowman's rare 1992 cards cost $270 per set. *Pictured:* 1992 Bowman Dino Hackett #32.

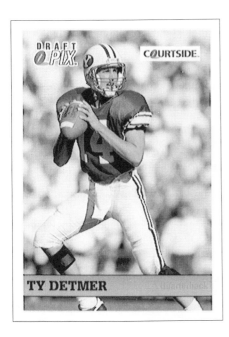

Allergy sufferers should be wary of 1992 Courtside cards, which reek of formaldehyde. *Pictured:* **1992 Courtside Ty Detmer #25.**

censes. What started out as fun got grim; 1992 saw the release of 22 mainline sets. Who could keep track of them all, let alone collect them?

By 1993 there wasn't much football card manufacturers could do to top 1992's landmark deluge of product.

As in 1992, the presses quit in 1993 after about two dozen new sets (the count varies, depending on how you decide to classify them). Entries such as CME's dog tags were difficult to categorize as football cards. They did have players on them, but, well, they were more like *dog tags* than anything else. Pro Line switched from the fashion cards of 1992 to standard football cards, with rookies and veteran stars included.

"busy" look of the cards. Perhaps Wild Card's set isn't perfect, but unlike Topps, at least they tried.

Wild Card is a strong new competitor in the card business with a singular trading scheme. Wild Card football cards are randomly marked with denomination stripes of 5, 10, 20, or more. A stripe card can be returned to the company for as many of the same card as the stripe shows. A small handling fee is also charged. Owners of Wild Card stripe cards in high denominations for star players have valuable items on their hands. Pack prices for 1992 Wild Card cards were a bargain at $1 each. This truly is an underrated set.

The NFL in 1992 did the hobby a disservice by granting so many li-

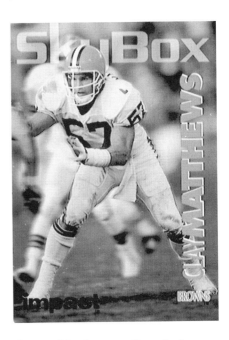

The NFL did collectors a disservice by granting so many licenses in 1992. *Pictured:* **1992 SkyBox Impact Clay Matthews #63.**

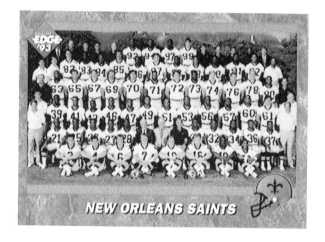

After 1992 there wasn't much card makers could do to match that year's deluge of product. *Pictured, counterclockwise from top:* 1993 Collector's Edge New Orleans Saints #137, 1993 Upper Deck Dan Marino #150, and 1993 Score Pinnacle Steve Young #255.

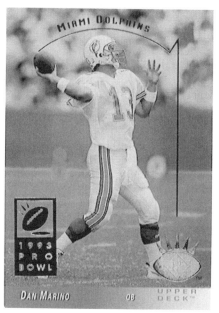

On other football card fronts, successful makers weighed in with their usual glitzy stuff.

Collector's Edge, famous for plastic card stock, increased the number of items in its set from 175 to a 1993 total of 250 cards. The odd black borders from 1992 were replaced by a more attractive marbled look.

Fleer assumed control of Game-Day but kept the number of cards in the set at 500. Fleer also kept the large GameDay card size and added a splash of extra color to card fronts.

Fleer's 500-card regular 1993 issue was an improvement over prior substandard material. For this issue collectors were willing to pay double

GameDay has flattered Action Packed by imitating the sculpted look on some of its 1994 cards. *Pictured:* 1994 GameDay Rookie Trev Alberts #2.

leased three other sets—Rookies, All Madden, and a new *Monday Night Football* set. Of the three, the rookie set is likely to provoke the greatest long-term collector interest.

Other noteworthy 1993 releases included sets by SkyBox, Pro Set, Playoff, Wild Card, Upper Deck, Pinnacle, Topps, and Pacific.

As usual Topps issued two sets, a regular set and the premium Topps Stadium Club set. The regular Topps set is not as bad as previous efforts. Topps Stadium Club went from 700 cards in 1992 to a mere 550 cards in 1993. The quality was as good or better than previous Stadium Club releases.

But the sameness of design is widely counted as a strike against

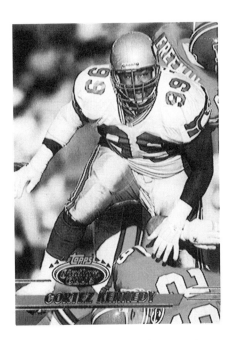

Sameness of design is widely counted against the Topps Stadium Club product. *Pictured:* 1993 Topps Stadium Club Cortez Kennedy #45.

what they were willing to pay for the earlier issue. In 1993 the 1992 Fleer set was still selling for $8. The 1993 regular Fleer set ranged from $16 to $20.

Fleer's 1993 Ultra set was praised for great player selection and a superior design. A whole bunch of 10-card insert subsets rounded out 1993 Fleer Ultra.

Action Packed reduced the number of cards in its regular premium set to 162. To take up the slack, it re-the Topps Stadium Club product. Sameness can be a sign of either consistency or lack of imagination. Topps Stadium Club is not exactly stylish. It's dull and has a shopworn look. Many football card collectors have been eager to reward Topps for finally getting with the program and issuing a premium set like others in the hobby. That's why Topps 1992 Stadium Club still fetches a price well above $100. No other 1992 premium set is worth as much. But it's a so-so product.

The Topps brand commands the loyalty of many football card collectors because of the long history the company has in the hobby. However, the cards themselves don't necessarily rate the collector's approval. Better cards are made by other companies.

Three card sets surpassing the Topps Stadium Club set in 1993 were Playoff, SkyBox NFL, and Upper Deck SP.

The 1993 Playoff cards are an interesting lot. The patented Tekchrome photography is an innovation similar to the GameDay color/monochrome image combination. But Playoff carries the technique a step further by giving the color part of the player photo a silverish sheen. Hold Playoff cards up to the light and see the player jump out at you.

SkyBox again did all the right things in its NFL set. Plenty of rookies are interspersed throughout a galaxy of established stars. It's everything a premium set ought to be and more. Football card investors looking for rookie singles to gamble on might well check out 1993 SkyBox NFL.

It is useful to note the difference between SkyBox 1993 NFL and SkyBox 1993 Impact. SkyBox NFL is a good premium card set. SkyBox Impact is not. For the second year in a row, SkyBox issued two card sets with widely varying quality and selection. Do yourself a favor and ignore Impact.

Upper Deck SP is a 270-card set with features many collectors seem to like. In essence, it's not all that different from other premium sets, but it can't be faulted for that. It has important rookie cards collectors seek and claimed top spot among all the 1993 sets as most valuable, selling for $80 at year's end.

Pro Set and Pacific are regular-issue football cards that set fairly high standards for what are generally medium-range football cards. The place where Pro Set scores, as always, is in its extraordinary photography. The 449-card Pro Set regular issue covers most bases anyone would expect from a set of football cards but doesn't go much beyond. The player selection is adequate, but by putting out fewer cards than in the 1991 and 1992 sets, Pro Set isn't going out on a limb.

Pacific 1993 was a pedestrian set any way you look at it. Angled photos on the card fronts do little but make for a cockeyed design, and the marbled look on the borders has been done better by others, notably Collector's Edge.

So it is not surprising that Pacific had to set itself apart with a new premium issue. The vehicle of choice was Pacific Prisms, a 108-card premium set so pricey that the cards came one to a pack. In 1992 Pacific had done a 10-card Prisms insert in its regular issue and decided it was popular enough to warrant a large-scale effort. The full set cost $200 by late 1994, making it not unlike the Topps Gold set, only more expensive.

Score 1993 was considered a good basic set. Companion Pinnacle

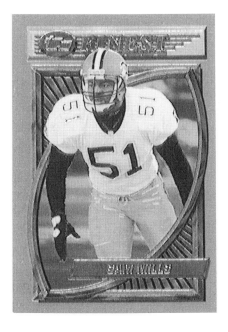

was written off quickly because there were no rookies in it other than a scarce 25-player rookie insert set. The rookies came with a price tag of $350 if you wanted them all. Longtime collectors like me wonder: Who really wants these things?

Topps started out 1994 by issuing the super premium Topps Finest set. By midsummer, player movement in the league had rendered many team associations on the Topps cards obsolete. But for once Topps had gotten the jump on the competition with a card so deluxe it appeared to be copying the Action Packed style.

The message must be that there is practically no limit to what the card companies will do to go their competitors one better.

Most recently we have seen the advent of the "chase card" phenomenon. Chase cards are insert cards scattered among the regular cards of a given set. Usually these insert cards are part of an ultra deluxe subset. The purpose of chase cards is to make collectors "chase" the special items.

Practically everybody went with chase cards in 1994: Action Packed

Topps also copied the Action Packed sculpted style with a new 1994 "Topps Finest" series. *Pictured:* **1994 Topps Finest Sam Mills #154 front and reverse.**

issued a 42-card Fantasy Forecast series, Classic a 45-card MVP Sweepstakes set, and Collector's Edge a 25-card Boss Squad, to name a few. Pacific took its Prisms cards from a 10-card 1992 chase subset to a full 126-card set in 1994. In football card collecting, it's not just collectors who rush en masse to the latest thing—manufacturers do it too.

Though even the most dedicated football card collectors can't follow all the available sets, it is flattering that our hobby has aroused so much free market competition. While it is a headache to have so many football cards, we might take the long view and remember that there may be some authentic investment gems here. In time we could be looking at the 1990s as a pivotal era in the development of the football card hobby and maybe see some of these cards grow quite valuable.

If only we knew in advance which ones they would be.

CHAPTER ELEVEN

THE NEW GOLDEN AGE OF FOOTBALL CARDS

Why Now?

Modern football card collecting truly began with the issue of the 1948 Bowman and Leaf card sets. Baseball card collecting, by contrast, has had a continuous history reaching back more than 100 years.

As we have seen, two football card issues did come out before 1948 that merit interest. These are the 1890s Mayo Cut Plug set of college stars and the 1935 National Chicle set. But for the hobby as a whole, these sets exist outside the mainstream, available to the average collector only as reprints. The year 1948 marks the time football card collecting began in earnest.

After 1948 the history of the hobby can be divided into three major periods. The first ran from 1948 to 1955 and is notable for the release of Bowman's string of classic sets. The second period began in 1956 when Topps entered the market, successfully fended off challenges from both Fleer and Philly Gum, and became the sole producer of football cards from 1968 to 1988. The third period opened in 1989 with the advent of Score, Pro Set, and Action Packed cards. All three outshined Topps

with new and improved designs. Football cards had finally arrived, turning a forgotten hobby corner into the glamour sector of the trading card industry.

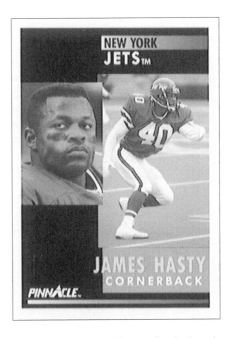

After the revolution of 1989, football cards became the glamour sector of the trading card industry. *Pictured:* 1991 Score Pinnacle James Hasty #162.

Suddenly, what seemed like a thousand flowers bloomed.

Each year since 1989, the hobby has brought forth more fabulous material. We are awash in riches. With yearly releases now running into double digits, informed collectors know that today we are truly in the golden age of football card collecting.

By December 1992, football card manufacturers had swamped collectors with 20 major NFL card sets, two World League sets, and two Canadian sets, along with a whole slew of specials, rookies, and updates. For football card collectors, 1992 was the blowout, the limit. No matter how much we may like football and enjoy card collecting, 1992 was overwhelming. It proved that even

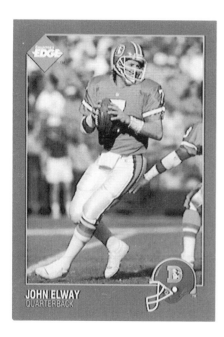

By 1992 the two-digit trend in football sets (at least ten sets released each year) was well-established. *Pictured:* 1992 Collectors Edge John Elway #37.

diehard collectors can get too much of a good thing.

It is interesting that our long-neglected hobby has aroused so much attention; in fact, it's both flattering and troubling. We ask ourselves: When will the bottom fall out? Can this go on forever? And why on earth this sudden deluge of football cards?

Like most things in professional sport in the United States, the sports card surge originated with baseball. As the oldest professional team sport in America, baseball is where new things happen first. The explosion of interest in sports cards started over a decade ago on the baseball side of the card-collecting hobby.

The Topps monopoly in baseball was broken in the early 1980s rather than in the late 1980s, as it was in football. Over in baseball, both Fleer and Donruss gained the rights to make baseball cards as early as 1981, and later they were joined by Score, Sportflics, and glossy newcomers like Upper Deck and Leaf. As a privately held, secretive company with a substandard product, Topps stayed resolutely behind the times until the advent of Stadium Club in 1991.

Collectors were thrilled by baseball cards in the 1980s, enjoying many superb sets. An example is the coveted 1984 Donruss baseball set, which today retails for about $300. In the same way that player free agency came first to baseball and later to football, baseball's wide-open card scene also spread to football.

But there are differences in the two hobbies. It seems that baseball card collectors are a more conservative, less fickle lot than football card

collectors. As a group, they are ac-
quisitive rather than speculative. In
baseball, collectors seek cards of
their favorite teams or players and
treasure them. The football card collector is more given to wild swings of
affection, buying up cards of today's
hero and ditching that same hero
when he is supplanted by another.

Like Bo Jackson. Two years after
his hip injury, the Jackson card was
listed at just over two bucks. Now it
is worth only a dime. After receiving
an artificial hip, Jackson has continued to play professional baseball.
Most of us who follow sports admire
his courage if not his wisdom.

Today Jackson's football card is
practically worthless. Do collectors
lose their enthusiasm for a player
who gets hurt?

Yes! In football, players are one
injury away from oblivion.

About the only thing football
card collectors don't seem to lose is
enthusiasm for the game itself.

The NFL mystique is irresistible.
In many towns kids dressed in Los
Angeles Raiders gear hang around
the mall, smoking cigarettes and act-
ing tough. But the mystique is successful in spite of rather than because
of the NFL. The NFL is a hard outfit
to fathom. It presents a stone face to
the public, driving away potential
spectators with a value system that
holds money above loyalty to any
city, team, or even the fans.

It's the kind of arrogance that always leads to a fall.

But there's no doubt football is a
natural for cards, the perfect sport to
depict on those little slips of collectible cardboard. This may be the
golden age of all sorts of trading

The NFL mystique is irresistible. Kids hang
around the mall, dressed in Los Angeles
Raiders gear. *Pictured:* 1993 Skybox Impact
Nick Bell #151.

cards, but let us remember that primarily cards are pictures of people
and the things people do. There
aren't many better subjects for people photography than the high-
speed, violent game of football.

In football, guys not only hit and
run and throw, they try to batter each
other into submission. They dive,
they jump, they kick. They fly to the
ball. Helmets crash and guys get cov-
ered with sweat, dirt, and blood. It is
quite simply the ideal sport for stag-
ing contests of courage and aggres-
sion. Moreover, the tightly choreo-
graphed action sequences of football,
like those made famous by the Dallas
Cowboys, lend themselves ideally to
the talents of sports photographers.

Fans who watched the Cowboys

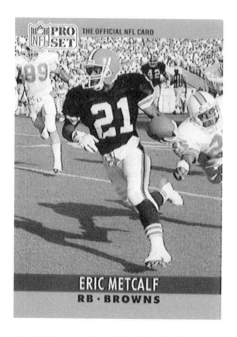
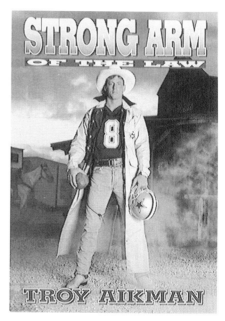

Football is considered the ideal action sport by many professional photographers. *Pictured, from left to right:* **1990 Pro Set Eric Metcalf #74 and 1992 PrimeTime Troy Aikman #313.**

in the 1970s always enjoyed the absolute precision that marked the Dallas offensive line play. Coach Tom Landry's teams were famous for their mastery of the art of controlled violence. Unfortunately for Landry, the decline of his scouting apparatus eventually led to his ouster.

But Landry's teams were among the best drilled and most disciplined in professional football.

Lucky for Dallas fans, they again got to see vintage Cowboy football in an updated version by watching the Jimmy Jones edition of the team in the early 1990s.

A good reason for many to get interested in the hobby is that not only has the volume of new material increased, but the quality has jumped as well. Five years ago a set like the

1991 Action Packed set was inconceivable. Critics of the high-end sets say that cards should be low-priced so kids can afford them. While that point is valid, much of the best current material is still within the reach of younger collectors. Typically, a pack of Score or Wild Card cards goes for under a buck. Collecting them all may be pricey, but that's what birthdays and factory sets are for.

The American craze for collecting goods of all kinds is no doubt partly responsible for the boom in football issues. But high interest in the sport and the end of the Topps monopoly have combined to make football cards a sure-fire winner.

According to industry sources, about 3.3 million people collect football cards. Makers turned about $150 million in gross sales in 1992, the best year ever. One set of the many issued in 1992 illustrates how the numbers work: SkyBox PrimeTime limited production in 1992 to 10,000 cases. The entire production sold out in about a month. Ten boxes filled each case, and each box held 36 foil packs of cards. The foil packs usually sold retail for $1.75 each. Thus, each box represented a sale of $63. Every case was therefore worth $630 retail and 10,000 cases earned dealers over $6 million.

Collectors should remember that other outfits were not nearly so fru-

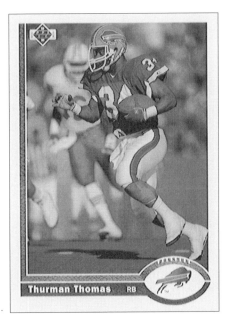

Collectors know that a colorful, well-made card is like a piece of the action. *Pictured:* 1991 Upper Deck Thurman Thomas #356.

Years ago a set with the production values and good looks of the 1991 Action Packed was inconceivable. *Pictured:* 1991 Action Packed Rookie Ed McCaffrey #23.

gal in their 1992 card production as PrimeTime. It's those overproduced cards that drive down values, a problem that SkyBox sought to avoid with limited production.

Football cards may represent just a small part of the national collecting mania, but they are a fascinating outgrowth of our enthusiasm for what is now the national sport. You can see your favorite player at the stadium or watch him play on TV.

Then he can appear in the palm of your hand. Smart collectors and manufacturers know a colorful, well-made card provides the committed fan with a keepsake, a true piece of the action.

SPECIAL CATEGORIES OF CARDS

CHAPTER TWELVE

NORTH COUNTRY FOOTBALL

Canadian League Cards 1952–1992

Canadian football cards celebrated a four-decade anniversary in 1992. From the earliest known Parkhurst issue in 1952 to the modern All World and Jogo offerings, Canadian football has given card collectors a wide variety of quality material.

Adding more interest to CFL cards is the Canadian Football League's major U.S. invasion in 1993, when club owners placed a team in Sacramento, California. In late 1993 the league announced plans for three more U.S. teams to begin play in 1994 in Las Vegas, Baltimore, and Shreveport, Louisiana. Because of these developments, all North American football card hobbyists may find an overview of CFL cards both old and new worthwhile.

Sports entrepreneur Bruce McNall has spearheaded broad changes in the CFL. The league has embarked on a bold program of expansion that aims to bring in large segments of the fan population south of the border.

But how to attract top talent is one of the intriguing problems facing Canadian Football League owners in the 1990s. Toronto Argonauts owner McNall saw his player contract and his multimillion dollar personal services deal with Raghib "Rocket" Ismail expire in 1993. Ismail hired sports agent Bob Woolf to cut a contract for him with the Los Angeles Raiders, who had picked Ismail in the 1991 NFL draft.

"If Ismail doesn't sign with the Raiders," McNall said at the time, "he'd still be one of our star players and we'd pay him commensurate with that. But I'm not going to allow the Raiders to take advantage of a situation where they have a monopoly."

McNall was whistling in the dark. Woolf eventually put together a two-year, $3 million pact with the Raiders that put Ismail on the Silver and Black roster to stay.

Previously a sideshow to the NFL, the Canadian Football League has shown real spunk by invading territory long dominated by the NFL. As a result, a new and larger audience of collectors may be pondering the purchase of CFL trading cards.

There are pros and cons to the Canadian game itself, which has only three downs and so is a far different game than the brute force drama favored in the NFL. In the card hobby, Canadian issues also exhibit significant differences.

Canadian Football League professional football cards appeared four years after postwar professional football cards for the NFL. In the NFL, the first postwar cards appeared in 1948. The first CFL cards

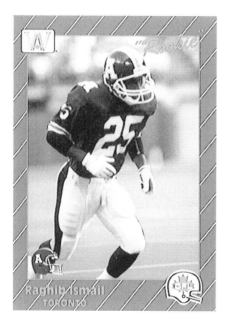

arrived in 1952 and were produced by the Parkhurst company, then as now makers of well-regarded hockey card sets.

The first Parkhurst set contained 100 somewhat small cards, measuring 1⅞" by 2¾". The front photos are black-and-white. The Parkhurst cards are proportioned like modern cards, most of which measure 2½" by 3½". The first 19 cards in the set are instructional cards, and the remainder focus on players in four CFL teams. This is a rare and rather valuable CFL set, priced at about $2,000 if it can be found for sale. The 1952 Parkhurst cards are almost never seen in the United States.

The next set chronologically is the 1954 CFL set made by Blue Ribbon Tea. It's an 80-card color set originally designed to go into a special album. Six teams are represented in the set: the Montreal Alouettes, the Winnipeg Blue Bombers, the Hamilton Tiger-Cats, the Ottowa Rough Riders, the Edmonton Eskimos, and the Calgary Stampeders. The backs are written in French and English.

This is a rare and attractive set

Attracting top talent like "Rocket" Ismail is one of the problems facing the Canadian Football League. *Pictured:* 1991 All World Raghib Ismail #92 front and reverse.

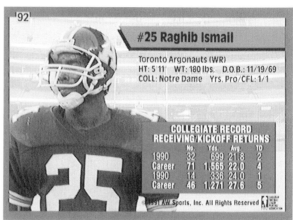

collectors find even harder to come by than the 1952 Parkhurst set. A complete set in near-mint condition could easily set a well-heeled collector back a cool $10,000. Unlike comparable NFL sets that break the four-figure mark, the value of the CFL Blue Ribbon Tea cards does not depend on heavyweight cards. Almost every card in the set, however, sells for about $100 in near-mint. This rather high across-the-board price accounts for the large cumulative total.

Two CFL card sets were issued in 1956—Parkhurst and Shredded Wheat. After a four-year hiatus, Parkhurst printed another CFL set, this time numbering 50 cards. The cards come arranged in subsets of ten players each, with five of the seven CFL teams represented.

The more ambitious 1956 Shredded Wheat set contains 105 cards, with players from all seven CFL teams. The teams included in this set are the Calgary Stampeders, the Edmonton Eskimos, the Winnipeg Blue Bombers, the Hamilton Tiger-Cats, the Toronto Argonauts, the Saskatchewan Roughriders, and the Ottawa Rough Riders.

It's an oddity of Canadian football that two of the teams have nearly identical nicknames. Many football fans south of the border have been confused by the difference between Saskatchewan's Roughriders and Ottawa's Rough Riders. Here in the United States, the business organization called the NFL is less accepting of duplicate team names than the freewheeling CFL.

The 1956 Shredded Wheat set has a nifty colored stripe behind the player's head in the picture on the card fronts. But otherwise the photography is black-and-white.

The 1959 Wheaties 48-card set would be considered a minor set if not for the dearth of Canadian cards. The cards are similar to the 1956 Shredded Wheat set, with backs written in both French and English.

Topps CFL sets are scarce. *Pictured:* **1963 Topps CFL Joe Kapp #3.**

The Wheaties cards are also nearly as rare as the earlier set, and the set is valued in near-mint at over $3,000.

From 1958 to 1965, Topps produced consecutive CFL sets. The first Topps CFL set in 1958 is virtually identical to the 1958 Topps NFL set, but it has only 88 cards rather than 132. The most valuable card in this CFL set, with a price of about $20, belongs to running back Cookie Gilchrist.

Gilchrist put eight seasons under his belt in the CFL before becoming the first 1,000-yard rusher in the history of the newly formed American Football League. Long-time pro fans familiar with the AFL know Cookie performed his 1,000-yard feat in Buffalo during the 1962 season.

All the rest of the Topps sets, from 1959 through 1965, have formats identical to their NFL counterparts. Topps usually grouped the cards in

Topps CFL cards all have the Topps "T.C.G." trademark but were actually printed in Canada. *Pictured:* 1963 Topps CFL B.C. Lions Team #10 front and reverse.

team order, and the only major difference between the NFL and the CFL sets is that there are always fewer cards in the CFL sets. For example, the 1963 Topps NFL set has 170 cards. The 1963 CFL set has 88. Another item of note is that the cards all have the Topps "T.C.G." trademark but were actually printed in Canada by the O-Pee-Chee Company.

Considered as a group, the Topps CFL sets are scarce but not as highly sought as NFL sets from the same years. Canada is a small country, with just over 20 million people. The United States is more than ten times larger. The smaller Canadian market limits the popularity of CFL cards.

CFL cards are generally not as valuable as NFL cards, but individual cards like the 1960 CFL Joe Kapp card are exceptions. Kapp went on to lead the Minnesota Vikings into Super Bowl IV, where they lost to the Kansas City Chiefs 23-7. He is an example of a former CFL player who gained sufficient exposure in the United States to make his Canadian card more valuable. There are a handful of such cards. Warren Moon's 1983 CFL card is a recent example of this phenomenon.

Other CFL cards from the 1960s deserving attention are the 1962 and 1963 Post Cereal CFL sets. In the NFL the Post sets are considered minor sets because Topps produced major NFL sets during the early 1960s. But the rare 1962 NFL set is still valuable; when it is found in near-mint condition, it can go for up to $4,000.

The two Canadian Post issues are nowhere near so pricey. The big reason is that the sets have no instantly recognizable stars.

Another reason that the 1963 Post CFL cards are less valuable is that they were made available to consumers in a different way than the 1962 Post set. The 1962 NFL and CFL Post sets were available only on the backs of cereal boxes. Cards from less popular cereals are pretty scarce. Those that are in general circulation are often crudely cut from the back of the box. It seems as though nobody thought to have the 1962 Post cards properly trimmed with a paper cutter.

The 1963 Post CFL cards, on the other hand, were available directly from Post's Canadian affiliate through a mail-in offer. This means that the 1963 Post CFL set of 160 cards is much more plentiful, especially in near-mint condition, than either of the other two. At $600 to $700, the 1963 Post CFL set is priced about half the 1962 Post CFL set of 137 cards. And it is only one-fifth the price of the 1962 Post NFL set, which has Don Meredith and a host of other major NFL names.

It's hard to see why anybody would get excited about any of the Post sets, CFL or NFL. They're not world-beaters as football cards. It is cute to see CFL player information written in both English and French, but that's about the only thing that sets these cards apart from any ordinary minor issue.

After Topps stopped making CFL cards in 1965, O-Pee-Chee took the baton and began producing its own CFL sets in 1968.

The first O-Pee-Chee set contained 132 cards, including a checklist. It appears to have been some sort of a test set because it received only scattered distribution in Canada and no distribution at all in the United States. The cards are similar to the Topps product of the same era, especially on the card fronts. The name and player position are printed in exactly the same style as on Topps NFL cards from 1968. The text on the card backs is written in both French and English.

These are fairly average cards as far as design is concerned, but the player selection is excellent. A full set is priced at nearly $1,000 in top-grade condition.

The next O-Pee-Chee set didn't appear until 1970 and featured 115 cards, five of which (numbers 111-115) are special cards listing an outstanding player, a 1970 player of the year, a lineman of the year, and CFL coaches. The fifth card explains how the uniform numbering system works in the CFL. This set also mimics the Topps product of the same year in design.

The 1971 O-Pee-Chee set is notable for having the first card of former Washington Redskin quarterback Joe Theismann as card #13. Theismann played in Canada for three years until he was brought south by Washington to understudy veteran quarterback Billy Kilmer. In Washington Theismann proved his toughness by returning punts on special teams until Kilmer's retirement. At $75 the Theismann card today represents about half of the value of the 1971 O-Pee-Chee set.

The 1972 O-Pee-Chee set was the last one for the company. Again O-Pee-Chee issued a set of 132 cards resembling the Topps NFL product of the same year. This is the least valu-

able and least interesting of the four O-Pee-Chee CFL issues. Just about all it has for collectors is Theismann's second card and CFL stars Johnny Musso, Ron Lancaster, and Granville Liggins.

The rest of the 1970s was a disappointing time for football card collectors in Canada. The only CFL set issued during the remainder of the decade was a minor set printed by potato chip maker Nalley's. This small 30-card set was distributed only in Western Canada and has just one player familiar to NFL fans in the United States. That player is Joe Pisarcik, a quarterback who had marginal success playing later for the New York Giants.

A new era in Canadian football card collecting was inaugurated when Jogo Novelties released its first CFL set in 1981. This set contained only 50 cards, but it featured a pleasing design despite simple production values. The front photos are all black-and-white, and the backs are printed in blue ink.

The 1981 Jogo set is a card collector's set, made for people who admire and enjoy the Canadian version of the game. It has no glitzy special features. It's just a nice little card series to serve literally and figuratively as a snapshot of the game.

This small set is notable for having the first professional card of quarterback Warren Moon.

Fresh out of the University of Washington, Moon went to Canada because offers from the NFL were paltry and few. In Canada Moon was eclipsed by nobody, winning consecutive championships at Winnipeg until he was persuaded to go south, where at last he was able to name his own terms.

In 1982 Jogo went full color, making a lively 24-card set devoted to players from the Ottawa Rough Riders only.

Throughout the 1980s Jogo provided CFL card collectors with sets that were noted for skillful player selection, moderate price, and good quality. The highly sought and exceptionally valuable 1983 Jogo Limited set is a good example.

A mere 600 numbered copies of this set were produced by the company. The 1983 Jogo Limited has the most valuable Warren Moon card by far, selling today for about $400. Moon is reputed to have bought large quantities of his 1983 card from Jogo to distribute to friends and fans.

As a result, the Jogo Limited set is the most valuable of all the Jogo CFL sets.

The Jogo effort peaked in 1991 with the release of a highly regarded 220-card set. The set is arranged according to teams and has a solid design. The black backs have yellow text that is quite attractive, and player selection is strong. Fully half the players in the CFL are on 1991 Jogo cards. In a nutshell, the 1991 Jogo offering is the best, most comprehensive CFL set ever issued.

Jogo's 1991 set had to be good, considering that another major player was stirring up the Canadian football card scene.

All World, a new company, beat out Jogo in 1991 for the card license of a hot new CFL star, Raghib

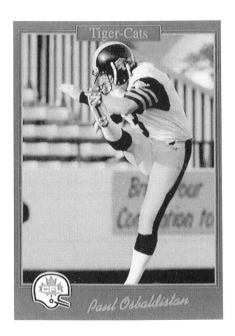 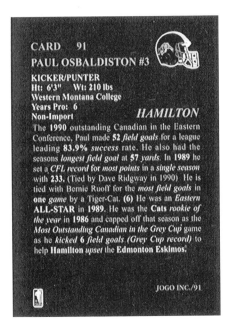

About half the players in the CFL are on the 1991 Jogo cards. *Pictured:* 1991 Jogo CFL Paul Osbaldiston #91 front and reverse.

"Rocket" Ismail. By signing Ismail to an exclusive contract, All World diverted much of the attention away from Jogo's fine 1991 set.

All World then exploited its coup by releasing not one but nine separate Rocket cards in its 110-card set.

You can hardly blame All World. Small, fast, and incredibly elusive, the Rocket is the prototype CFL receiver. In the CFL the offense is allowed only three downs to advance the ball the requisite ten yards. Unlike football as played in the NFL, the Canadian game emphasizes finesse over power.

The All World factory set came in two versions—English and French. Both were priced between $5 and $10 retail. At first collectors thought the most likely Rocket rookie card would be #1 in the AW CFL set.

Not so, said AW executive Erik Eckholm, who pointed out that All World had other ideas when it made up the set. "The 1991 All World CFL trading card set contained nine Ismail cards," Eckholm said. "The card we consider to be his rookie card is #92."

Collectors checking out the different rookie cards in All World's 1991 set will notice that the card number on the back of Ismail card #92 is highlighted in yellow, a clue that All World intended to make it his official rookie card.

In 1992 both Jogo and All World played in the Canadian Football League card market. Both made comprehensive CFL sets, although neither is easy to find in the United States.

So far, having CFL teams in the United States hasn't had much impact on card collectors. CFL card issues are no more popular in American markets today than they were before the Sacramento expansion team joined the league. But perhaps the cable TV package the CFL negotiated with all-sports channel ESPN2 will change American attitudes in the future.

The Sacramento Gold Miners, playing with personnel and coaches inherited from the defunct World League club, enjoyed only limited success in the 1993 CFL season.

The 1994 season saw Baltimore's CFL team make it to the Grey Cup final, the CFL equivalent of the Super Bowl. A nicknameless Baltimore franchise was narrowly defeated by the B.C. Lions in a memorable game.

Aggressive marketing techniques have slowly built a solid core of U.S. fans, and soon one of the new teams may achieve the ultimate success in the CFL—winning the Grey Cup.

But whatever happens as a consequence of the great Canadian invasion, it should provide new opportunities for football players and fans alike. Card collectors may also benefit.

CHAPTER THIRTEEN

THE TOPPS USFL SETS, 1984–1985

Upstart League Rates Quality Cards

The United States Football League came and went during a three-year period, playing spring seasons in 1983, 1984, and 1985. A planned autumn season in 1986 never materialized because the league collapsed. It fell victim to an adverse court decision and poor judgment by owners.

Not much remains. What does exist, as far as card collectors are concerned, are two superb, highly sought football card sets that have not only stood the test of time but have rocketed to the summit of modern-era collecting.

It wasn't always so. When the first USFL set came out, it was sold through hobby dealers and in the back pages of publications like *The Sporting News.* Ronald Chase, a card dealer at Oregon Sports Cards in Eugene, remembers when the 1984 USFL Premiere Edition boxed sets arrived at his store.

"At first we had a pyramid of USFL sets stacked up in the shop," Chase said. "It took a long time for them to sell out. I was charging $6.50 a box and not moving many. But by 1990 things had really changed."

Ronald Chase is not alone in his experience. In the past ten years, the way collectors view the USFL sets has changed dramatically. Originally just curios, the Topps USFL sets have become desirable items as the players pictured on the cards graduated

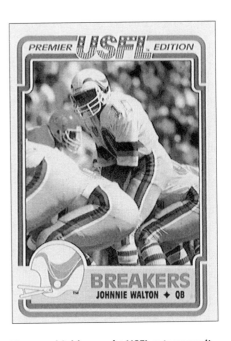

The now highly sought USFL sets weren't always so popular with collectors. *Pictured:* 1984 Topps USFL Johnnie Walton #82.

to the upper echelon of football stardom.

It may seem strange that while the Topps company was producing NFL football card sets of virtually no distinction, it should at the same time issue two excellent sets for a league that most fans shrugged off. But that's exactly what happened.

The Topps 1984 USFL Premier Edition 132-card set contains the true rookie cards of such pro notables as Jim Kelly, Reggie White, Herschel Walker, Steve Young, and Anthony Carter, to name a few. The 1984 checklist is loaded with recognizable names, in line with a USFL policy that allowed each roster several star-quality players in hopes of boosting fan interest in the new league. For collectors the result has been a football rookie card bonanza.

Topps supplied the 1984 set generally to hobby dealers like Chase as a potential collectible. It never received the mass market promotion afforded other Topps products, like the popular TV, sports, and film spinoff card sets. As noted, reaction at the time was pretty much a collective yawn. There were a few guys of NFL caliber included in the set, but the majority of the NFL veterans admittedly were past their prime or NFL second stringers—players like Matt Robinson, Raymond Chester, Arthur Whittington, Joe Gilliam, Glenn Carano, Vince Evans, Doug Plank, Cliff Stoudt, and Glenn Hyde.

But Topps had inexplicably produced a beautiful set, even though collectors disregarded it. The color schemes were vivid, the photography was well above average, and the

The Topps 1984 Premier Edition 132-card set is loaded with recognizable names. *Pictured:* 1984 Topps USFL Checklist #132 front and reverse.

lavender and blue card backs were a genuine innovation. On the fronts, most of the player pictures were action shots, a welcome departure from the standard Topps "Here-I-Am-Sweating-on-the-Bench" school of photography.

Collectors also failed to be interested in the fact that Topps included every single one of the USFL's top-money players. In addition to Kelly, Walker, and Young, the set included such names as Bobby Hebert, Ricky Sanders, Scott Norwood, Joe Cribbs, Kelvin Bryant, Irv Eatman, Gary Anderson, and Doug Williams.

For a time the Jim Kelly card drove the 1984 Premier Edition, not without justification. Kelly's card, #36 in the set, is in all respects a classic. The front shows Kelly wearing

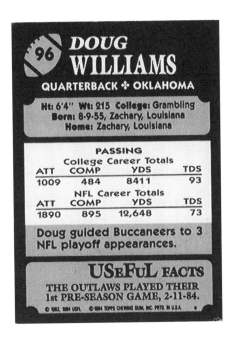

The lavender and blue card backs were a real innovation. *Pictured:* 1984 Topps USFL Doug Williams #96 reverse.

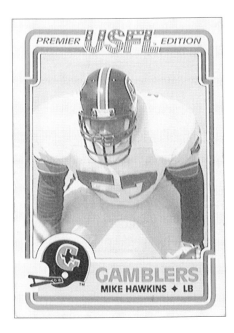

Topps had inexplicably produced a most beautiful set. *Pictured:* 1984 Topps USFL Mike Hawkins #35.

Houston Gambler whites, rolling out to pass in the run-and-shoot offense. Kelly has the ball at ready while he scans the field for an open man. One story has it that Topps gave Kelly 500 copies of the card from the original press run. As recently as November 1990, Kelly's card was rated the second most wanted card in the 1984 set. Until then Herschel Walker's was first.

As the 1984 USFL set began to really climb in price, Walker's card was still the major item, owing to his high visibility as running back for the Dallas Cowboys. In his first USFL season, Walker led the league in rushing. In his sophomore year, he finished a close second to Birmingham's Joe Cribbs. But in the NFL, Walker never attained the success he enjoyed playing for the USFL's New Jersey Generals. At least in the USFL they knew how to use this talented runner, handing off to him 20 to 30 times a game as workhorse for the Generals.

Walker's card, #74 in the Premier Edition set, was eclipsed by Kelly's card in 1991, no doubt because of the attention Kelly attracted from his Super Bowl appearances. Walker's card declined with his playing time. His 1991 duty as kick returner for the Minnesota Vikings broke the hearts of collectors everywhere. Walker's 1992 resurgence with the Philadelphia Eagles gladdened those same hearts. He was still able to tear off 100-yard rushing games with stunning regularity. As a result, the Walker card rebounded from an early 1992 low of $40 to a respectable $80 by December of that year.

Early 1995 saw the rapid ascent of the rookie card for 49er quarterback Steve Young. This gifted signal caller broke into pro football with the USFL Los Angeles Express. When the USFL folded, Young moved to the NFL, where he eventually wound up playing behind football legend Joe Montana in San Francisco.

Upon Montana's departure to Kansas City, Young won the starting job, and his card, #52 in the 1984 USFL set, began a steady rise. After leading San Francisco to victory in Super Bowl XXIX, the Young USFL rookie card zoomed over the $200 mark.

Beckett yearbooks for football cards from the 1980s show how interest in the 1984 USFL set climbed. In the 1987 Beckett book, the first in which the USFL set is listed, the price is a mere $15, about double its original retail price. It was a good price for such a recent set but not necessarily an omen of spectacular things to come.

The big jump occurred in 1989, when the price shot up to $50 for a mint 1984 USFL set. In about two years, it had nearly quadrupled in value. By any standard, that's a serious increase for a box of football cards, reflecting the NFL success of many former USFL players featured in the 1984 set.

Then the price in the 1990 Beckett book soars to $110, setting the stage for another phenomenal 1991 increase to $350. In 1992 the set added another hefty $100 to its value. What the future holds for this football high-flyer is impossible to guess, but probably more of the same. Today it is a very expensive set, and if you're dying to get your hands on one, you'll probably pay $400 to $500 in the current hobby market.

Two things make the 1984 set one of the best football card collectibles around. One is the attractiveness of the design—these are pretty cards, with above average photographic values and brilliant color. Topps executive Timm Boyle says that Topps policy prohibits releasing names of card designers or numbers of sets printed. In any event, the person or persons responsible did a class job.

Boyle discounts the persistent rumor that Topps gave Jim Kelly 500 copies of his rookie card. "I've talked to people who were around at the time," Boyle says, "and they tell me it isn't true."

But for collectors, the main consideration determining value in the 1984 Premier Edition set is the wide collection of superstars making their pro debut. The 1985 set, while not quite as attractive, follows up on rookies from the earlier set and adds a few more. Two signal examples are Heisman winners Mike Rozier and Doug Flutie.

Both the 1984 and the 1985 sets are complete at 132 cards. Of the two, the 1984 Premier Edition is the superior item. This set has to be considered outstanding work by Topps, not exceeded by any other Topps football product until the Stadium Club cards appeared in 1991.

The 1985 Topps USFL set is a reprise of the earlier set but is less attractive and uses colors less effectively. It does show the emergence of some authentic USFL stars. A typical example from the 1985 set is the rookie card of linebacker Sam Mills, now an NFL All-Pro with the New Orleans Saints. Fresh out of tiny Montclair State, Mills was considered too small and wasn't picked up in the 1981 NFL draft. But because Mills got a chance to prove himself in the USFL, he's gone on to be recognized by his peers, who voted for him to represent the NFC in the 1992 NFL Pro Bowl. In the USFL Mills was a stalwart of the Philadelphia Stars' "Doghouse" defense.

Also in the 1985 set is #80, Doug Flutie, who after a stint in the NFL is now a star quarterback in the CFL. In 1985 Flutie became signal caller for the New Jersey Generals after closing out his career at Boston College, where he was all-time collegiate passing leader.

Many former USFL players, in addition to the well-known stars, did well in the NFL. Once again it was

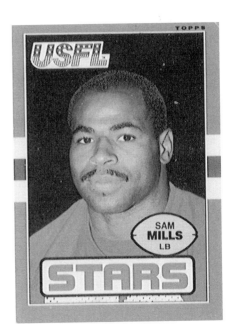

Many former USFL players did well in the NFL. *Pictured:* 1985 Topps USFL Sam Mills #19.

proven that while coaches, scouts, and front office types can measure a player's speed, strength, and agility, they still don't know how to measure his desire or his ability to win.

Critics of the USFL said that while it brought exciting football to the field, it was less successful in bringing fans to the gate. People simply weren't interested in spring football, and Mother's Day in particular is a bad day for a game. Critics also said that only one of the 12 original clubs, the Tampa Bay Bandits, was a solid financial success. Of course, much of the Bandits' success stemmed from the smart operation run by owner John Bassett, a master businessman. Unfortunately for the USFL, not all the owners had Bassett's professional acumen.

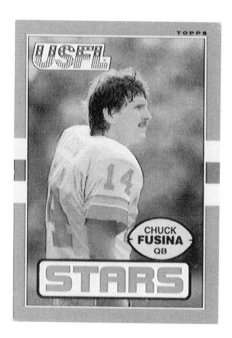

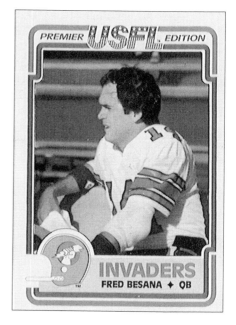

USFL champions the Philadelphia Stars were led by quarterback Chuck Fusina. *Pictured:* 1985 Topps USFL Chuck Fusina #15.

Many fans still miss the excitement of USFL games on balmy spring days and nights. *Pictured:* 1984 Topps USFL Fred Besana #84.

Bassett broke with the other USFL owners over the switch to a fall season, predicting it would be the end of the league. The one cool head in the group, Bassett was later proved right.

When you get right down to it, the USFL was killed by developer Donald Trump, who reportedly tried to use the threat of autumn competition with the NFL and a court suit to wedge his New Jersey Generals into the NFL. It was a ploy that just didn't work. Hundreds of mid-level players lost their jobs, while some 50 others migrated to the NFL.

On the field the primary focus of the USFL was the wide-open game, and here the USFL was a resounding success. For fans used to the conserv-

ative, defense-oriented NFL, the USFL had many genuine attractions. Even among USFL teams that did not feature the run-and-shoot, a common play on third and short was a bomb thrown straight down the middle.

Some great games were played in the USFL. Probably the most memorable contest took place in the first USFL playoff round in July 1983. The Philadelphia Stars, led by quarterback Chuck Fusina, put together a gutsy fourth-quarter rally to tie the Chicago Blitz. The Blitz was a team stocked with heady veterans from the NFL and coached by the late George Allen. The game went into overtime and the Stars won the coin toss.

In the extra period, running back Kelvin Bryant of the Stars scored on a 1-yard dive to win the game, 44-38. Afterward everyone associated with the game knew they'd been touched by greatness. Commenting on the loss, Coach Allen said: "A great game for the fans. Either team could have won. It will go down as one of the best games in history. My players played hard, and I told them I was proud of them."

Taking three Heisman winners in a row—Herschel Walker, Mike Rozier, and Doug Flutie—typified the go-for-broke style of pro football's best spring league. The USFL will forever remain a part of the storied history of professional football because it featured great games and great players. In retrospect, it was an idea perhaps a little ahead of its time.

In spite of all the years that have passed, many fans still miss the excitement of USFL football on balmy days and nights. The league is gone, but Topps did fans and football card collectors a big service by producing a pair of quality sets to highlight the brief existence of the USFL.

CHAPTER FOURTEEN

WORLD LEAGUE OF AMERICAN FOOTBALL

Pro Set, Ultimate, and Wild Card

In March 1991 the World League of American Football, created by the NFL, opened play with new teams from North America and Europe. A ten-game regular schedule and two playoff games culminated in a world championship. The June championship game was predictably designated the World Bowl. During 1991 Pro Set Inc. commemorated the World League season by releasing World League football cards in three separate series. Smart football card collectors have recognized that all three series exhibit many strengths and few flaws, showing early signs of becoming desired collectibles.

The 1991 Pro Set Series I packs contained 42 different World League cards, one to each pack. The bright, borderless cards were well-designed and showcased superior Pro Set photography. The cards were noted for their good graphics, readable text, and excellent color reproduction. Each team in the miniset was represented by a coach, a helmet card, and two players. A league president card and a game-opener card filled out the Series I issue.

Putting together a 42-card subset

from the Series I packs is difficult but not impossible. With a little luck, a resourceful collector should be able to do it for under $10.

The 1991 Pro Set Series II packs featured a nine-card World League leaders subset, numbered 703

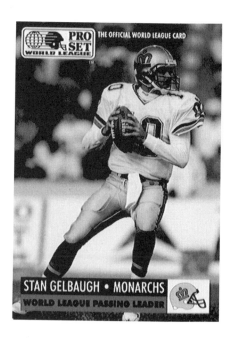

Pro Set's bright, borderless World League cards have superior photography. *Pictured*: 1991 Pro Set Stan Gelbaugh #704.

through 711. These cards highlighted the statistical leaders in various categories, such as passing, receiving, and rushing. Defensive players, including the three most valuable defenders—John Brantley, Anthony Parker, and Danny Lockett—finish the subset.

The third World League offering by Pro Set is the 150-card Inaugural Series Set, available in an attractively packaged four-set box. The individual sets come shrink-wrapped within a small red box with a sliding cover colored in purple and violet. A combined Pro Set/World League logo and text appear on the cover: "The Only Official Card of the World League." Although the sliding cover fits too loosely on the box, the 150 items inside make a nice little brick of cards.

All ten teams are represented in the boxed set by a mix of players. The mix provides a good idea of how the NFL stocked the fledgling league. Among the players are a number of guys who, for whatever reason, never quite cracked the first string in the big league. The rest of the cards feature untested players out of college and a scattering of Europeans. The European players arrived via Operation Discovery, a league project headed by John Ralston. For the 400 players who received the minimum 20 grand payment plus incentive bonuses, playing in the World League must have been one heck of a summer job.

The boxed set is clearly the standout collectible of the three Pro Set World League issues. It has five basic parts: The first three cards are a logo card, a fan card, and a first weekend

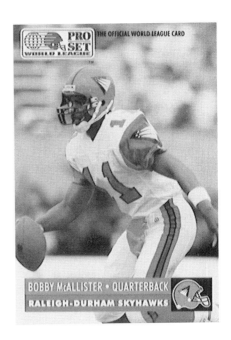

All ten World League teams were represented in the 1991 set by Pro Set. *Pictured: 1991 Pro Set World League Bobby McAllister #127.*

card. The following six relate to the World Bowl. Numbers 10-19 are helmet cards. Each team's helmet is shown on top of a map of the team's home location, just in case you are a little weak on geography. These cards duplicate the helmet cards inside the Series I packs, with one difference: In the boxed set, the helmet cards have the results of games and attendance figures on the reverse side. The helmet cards in the Series I packs list the play date instead. The Series I cards also have the words "World League Collectible" or "WL Helmet Collectible" on the card backs, and the helmet cards in the boxed set do not.

After the helmet cards in the boxed set, there is a stat leader sec-

The Pro Set helmet cards show each team's helmet on a map over the home location. *Pictured:* 1991 Pro Set London Monarchs Helmet Card #13.

players than others. The London Monarchs have the most with 18 cards. Three clubs tie for fewest with nine—the Raleigh-Durham Skyhawks, the Montreal Machine, and the Sacramento Surge. It appears that the NFL created the league to have somebody for the two flagship clubs, the London Monarchs and the New York–New Jersey Knights, to play against.

As in all Pro Set products, the photography on the card fronts is almost faultless. Probably the best single photo is #33 in the boxed set, Bruce Clark of the Barcelona Dragons, shown celebrating a sack of Birmingham's Eric Jones with a clenched fist and a broad smile. The least effective picture is most likely that of Tim

tion, highlighting the best individual performances in passing, rushing, returns, scoring, and defense. This section has some different categories than the leader section of Pro Set Series II. The 150-card boxed set has leaders for scoring (an honor shared by Orlando receiver Byron Williams and New York–New Jersey running back Eric Wilkerson), punting, kickoff returns, and punt returns. The Series II packs don't include these four categories but substitute a coach of the year, a World Bowl MVP, and a tri-defensive MVP.

From card #30 on in the boxed set, the stars of the ten teams are arranged in subsets, with the coach of each team occupying the last card. Some teams have more featured

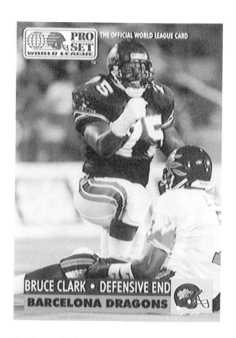

The best single photo in Pro Set's release is Bruce Clark of the Barcelona Dragons. *Pictured:* 1991 Pro Set World League Bruce Clark #33.

Broady, #59 in the boxed set. The grainy photo makes it look as if he's running away from the cheerleaders.

A major drawback to the boxed set and, incidentally, to all Pro Set football products, is that to get a checklist you have to request it from the company. The checklist arrives in the mail three weeks later as part of a catalog from Pro Set. Most collectors prefer a numbered checklist included with the set.

Another complaint I had was that the set I bought unopened did not contain a #4, the World Bowl Trophy card. However, I did get two #120's, the Byron Williams card. Byron is a good receiver, but I should have gotten a World Bowl Trophy card. Eventually, Pro Set courteously supplied a new World Bowl Trophy card to replace the missing one.

The investment value of a boxed set is hurt when it lacks a card. Without the Trophy card, a dealer purchasing the set would have to break it up to make a profit on the deal.

The boxed set gets, and deserves, most of the attention collectors give to the three 1991 Pro Set World League sets. This 150-card deluxe version is still available for $5 to $15 per individual boxed set. A 1991 Pro Set World League box contained four boxed sets and can be had for about $30. At that price, it's a sound investment. Football card values invariably rise along with the career of a player. There are a lot of young players with tremendous potential featured on the World League cards.

Might Pro Set World League cards be a good investment? The answer is yes. The number of companies putting out NFL cards has now

reached double digits, a quantity unthinkable five years ago. Considering what's happened in baseball cards during the last decade, collectors wonder why it took so long. After a while, though, even fanatic collectors tire of seeing the same players over and over. It's a pleasure to see something unusual, cards for a new league and new teams.

World League teams have well-chosen, exotic names. The Barcelona Dragons. The Frankfurt Galaxy. The New York–New Jersey Knights. World League cards also show off a lot of new faces, and the boxed set delivers more than 70 true rookie cards. Granted, many of these faces were never seen again. One of the ten

The two flagship clubs of the WLAF, the Monarchs and the New York–New Jersey Knights, did well against the rest of the league. *Pictured:* 1991 Pro Set World League Mouse Davis #110.

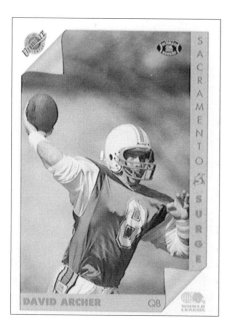

Ultimate made a World League set of its own in 1992. *Pictured:* 1992 Ultimate World League David Archer #144.

Ultimate's World League cards are packaged in a unique "Coliseum" box. The box opens to reveal 12 foil packs, one hologram sticker, and a miniposter. Every box has a built-in space that holds up to 200 cards, the equivalent of an entire set. The cards are excellent, with the player photographs laid out on the card fronts as if two corners of the picture were peeling, like posters on a sun-bleached fence. In the upper left corner is the Ultimate Company trademark. The lower right corner has the trademark of the World League. Throughout the set, the photography is uniformly good.

Ultimate's World League release has a few small drawbacks. It's hit-or-miss whether you get the correct number of cards in the foil packs. Each pack is supposed to contain nine cards. In three Coliseum boxes, I got two packs with 11 cards, one with six cards, and another pack with only four cards. In addition, the hologram is of poor quality, flimsy and not particularly vivid. Some dealers also complained that Ultimate pegged the wholesale price too high. An average price was $1.25 retail for nine cards, more if you figure that some packs were likely to be short a few cards.

However, within two years of release, boxes of the Ultimate World League cards sold at clearance sales for under $2.

At least one published report stated that Ultimate produced 2,000 cases of World League factory sets for distribution in the United States. However, the marketing department at Ultimate says this is false. "Ultimate printed no World League fac-

original clubs folded following the 1991 season. After posting a 0-10 record in 1991 under coach Roman Gabriel, the Raleigh-Durham Skyhawks called it quits. They were replaced in 1992 by the Ohio Glory, a team from Columbus. The footnote the Skyhawks made in the pro football history book is recorded practically nowhere but on the cards.

During the 1992 WLAF season, the Ultimate Trading Card Company marketed a second World League set, timing the appearance of the cards to the start of play in March 1992. Ultimate is owned by Smokey Scheinman, proprietor of Smokey's Card Shop in Las Vegas. The Ultimate set is clean and attractive, matching and in some ways exceeding the prior effort by Pro Set.

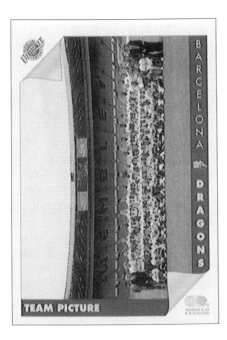

Ultimate World League boxes sold at clearance sales for under $2. *Pictured:* **1992 Ultimate World League Barcelona Dragons #17.**

by offering trades on numbered stripe cards. Just about everyone involved in the trading card hobby agrees that Wild Card's gimmick is a pretty good one. Here's how it works:

Randomly inserted in Wild Card's World League packs are certain cards marked by striped denominations on the lower left card front. The denomination cards could be sent back to Wild Card for the designated number of that same card (though without stripes). Smaller denominations could be combined and exchanged for larger ones, also. For example, Wild Card would send you a 100-stripe card for five 20-stripe cards. The ideal situation is to wind

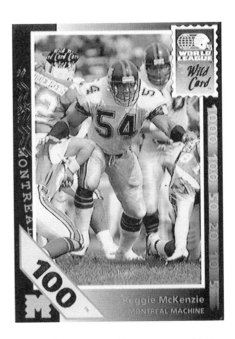

During the season, collectors were able to trade in their Wild Card stripe cards for the number of regular cards indicated in the "stripe." *Pictured:* **1992 Wild Card 100-stripe World League Reggie McKenzie #11.**

tory sets," said Debra Dasse at Smokey's headquarters in Las Vegas.

In summary, despite some relatively minor drawbacks, Ultimate delivered a very good World League football set, superior in some ways to a solid 1991 Pro Set World League release.

Wild Card entered the market with its own World League set in mid-1992, timing the appearance of the cards to the World League championship game at the end of the spring season. Wild Card is noted for its groundbreaking NFL and collegiate card sets, in addition to its unique promotional gimmick.

Wild Card's World League set follows in the footsteps of its NFL set

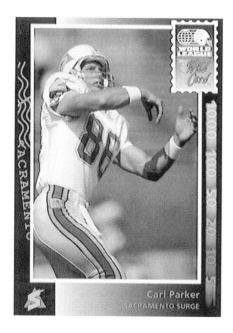

Instead of specials, Wild Card concentrated on making player cards. *Pictured:* **1992 Wild Card World League Carl Parker #47.**

onship card and the last three cards are checklist cards. All 146 remaining cards are player cards, ranging from NFL old-timers like defensive end Bruce Clark of the Barcelona Dragons to fresh rookies like quarterback Chris Cochrane of the Ohio Glory.

Wild Card's World League cards are packaged in extremely attractive black foil packs. Retailing at $1.50 per pack for 15 cards, they were a very good deal, considering Wild Card's quality and the scarcity of this issue in the marketplace.

The 1992 World League season was the story of how a lower echelon club, the Sacramento Surge, won the championship on the arm of a supposed NFL has-been, David Archer.

Archer, a former Atlanta Falcon

up with a highly regarded quarterback or running back in a large denomination. Wild Card stripes for such players often sell for top dollar in hobby shops. For a time, Todd Marinovich's 20-stripe NFL Wild Card rookie fetched upwards of $15.

Even without the denomination cards, Wild Card's entry in the World League card competition is close to perfect. Overall the set contains 150 cards, just about the right number for the league and identical to the number of cards Pro Set released in 1991. Wild Card differs from the Pro Set issue in a number of important ways. For one thing, Wild Card left out the coach cards and the helmet specials, concentrating instead on the players. In Wild Card's set, the first card is a 1991 champi-

Many players who eventually made it to the NFL can be found in the Wild Card World League set. *Pictured:* **1992 Wild Card World League Scott Mitchell #67.**

quarterback, generated big numbers at the position before giving way to Chris Miller. Archer signed with the World League in 1992 to help generate NFL interest in his flagging career.

"Most of the people around the NFL think alike," Archer said during a World Bowl halftime interview. "I joined the World League to see if I could change their minds about me."

Archer created a sensation by taking the Surge to the World Bowl, throwing repeatedly to receivers like "Downtown" Eddie Brown and former Vanderbilt star Carl Parker. The beefed-up Surge defense also helped turn 1991's lowly 3-7 club into champions.

It was a victory that raised the hopes of underdogs in all fields. Archer's card, #50 in the Wild Card set, is the key card to own. Other desirable cards are #67 Scott Mitchell, #91 Tony Baker, #107 Shawn Moore, and #36 Amir Rasul.

Wild Card's World League set is simply the best World League set available. It is clearly superior to the very fine 1991 Pro Set World League factory set and even a notch better than the flashy 1992 World League set by Ultimate. Football card collectors shouldn't ignore the possibility that there could be a windfall down the line if they add WLAF cards to their collections. Like the other two World League sets, the Wild Card set is loaded with rookies, some of whom have potential for stardom in the big league.

In September 1992 the NFL announced the suspension of the World League of American Football. Not only did the NFL put more than 400 football players out of work, but it also backed away from a historic experiment in international sports. Right after announcing the cancellation of the 1993 season, NFL officials said that the WLAF might be revived again in an altered form. Early in 1993, after NFL owners came to terms with players on the free agency issue, plans were announced for the eventual resumption of a Europe-only World League.

Could a future Hall of Famer be lurking in the World League football sets? Recall that Johnny Unitas went from $6 a game with a semipro team, the Bloomfield Rams, to stardom after he was picked up by the Baltimore Colts in 1956. They say it can happen to anybody with guts, luck, and the desire to make it.

It's possible future NFL stars are hiding there among the World League rookie cards.

But so far, not many collectors are betting on it.

CHAPTER FIFTEEN

HOAXES, ODDBALLS, AND ERROR CARDS

A Guide to Careful Collecting

HOAXES

It may be hard to believe that an activity like collecting football cards is subject to the kind of hoax that preys on human gullibility. But it happens all the time. Often the belief is rooted in some flimsy bit of evidence, like the vague resemblance one person may bear to another or a similarity in names. Solid research is the effective antidote to these delusions.

At least two major hoaxes are afoot in the football card hobby. The first concerns card #389 in the 1979 Topps football set. The player pictured on the card front is Ed O'Neil, an All-American at Penn State who for six years played with the Detroit Lions as linebacker and for one year played with Green Bay. On Thanksgiving Day 1977, O'Neil scored a touchdown while playing for the Lions.

Many people in the football card hobby believe that former Lion linebacker Ed O'Neil is the same person as Ed O'Neill of *Married . . . With Children* TV fame. So persistent has this rumor become that card #389 in the 1979 Topps set is becoming difficult to find. And it will sell for $15 on

up from those increasingly rare dealers who have a copy they're willing to part with.

Fans of the Fox show *Married . . . With Children* know Ed O'Neill as Al Bundy, the disgruntled shoe sales-

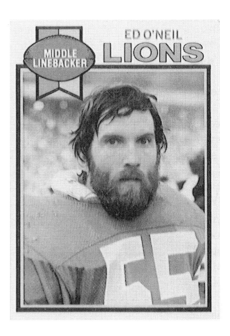

The Ed O'Neil hoax caused an obscure card to soar in price to $15. Is this guy really Al Bundy? *Pictured:* 1979 Topps Ed O'Neil #389.

man who fondly remembers his prowess as a high school football star. Al is a failure whose dream of being a football hero ended when he married Peggy, the mother of his smart-aleck children, Kelly and Bud. In one episode, Al Bundy says: "If I hadn't married Peggy, I could have gone to college, maybe even had a shot at the pros. I coulda been *somebody!*"

Abraham Lincoln, who knew people well, observed that you can fool some of the people all of the time. Today the easily fooled people believe Ed O'Neil and Ed O'Neill are the same guy.

But they aren't.

The Ed O'Neil card hoax briefly snared Jim Weir of All Pro Sportscards in Bellvue, Washington. "We had his card on the wall with a picture from the show until I took it down. Look closely and you can tell it's not the same guy," Weir said.

I asked him if he knew how the hoax got started.

"No, but I did some research and learned that the TV guy had a pro tryout but never played and never had a card."

When contacted by phone in Hollywood, the agent of the TV Ed O'Neill, Sheran Magnusson, confirmed that the actor was never a pro football player. "Ed once had a tryout with the Pittsburgh Steelers," Magnusson said, "but he never played professional ball."

The real Ed O'Neil, as far as football card collectors are concerned, was formerly an assistant coach with the Rutgers football team in New Brunswick, New Jersey.

"This came up a few years ago when that TV show got started," O'Neil said. "Somebody in Warren, Pennsylvania, which is my hometown, wrote the newspaper asking if I was now in television. The similarity in our names may have had something to do with it. But my last name is spelled with one 'l' rather than two. Since then, it's come up a few more times."

O'Neil talked about his professional career.

"I played six years in Detroit pretty much injury-free, from 1974 to 1979. In Green Bay I got hurt—knee and shoulder. The physical pounding was taking a toll. I had three children I wanted to be able to play with as they grew. My wife and I agreed it was time to hang it up. After the 1980 season, I retired."

Ed O'Neil finds it ironic that his card is hot in the hobby because people confuse him with the actor. "My family has a copy of the 1979 card and sometimes they tease me about it. You know, because the picture shows me in long hair and a beard. Don't I look great?"

The football Ed O'Neil says he's glad he got out of the game when he did.

"I feel sorry for guys who didn't know when to quit, guys who are so beat up they can hardly walk. They have only themselves to blame. We are intelligent people. We should know when to get out."

So, after a successful seven-year career, O'Neil put away the pads and got on with the rest of his life. His football card, the only one ever issued for him, is typical of football cards the hobby regards as commons. There's nothing wrong with commons. Commons are the most frequently found type of mainstream football card. Stars who gain the limelight in the blue-collar game of football are few and far between. Not even ultra-dedicated fans can usually name more than half a dozen players on a professional team outside their own city. That leaves a lot of room for lunch-bucket players who play, stop when it's time to stop, and move on.

Besides, it's something special for a football player in the 1970s, during the era of the Topps monopoly, to have any kind of card. Millions of middle-aged men in America would have loved being professional players and would relish the bonus of a picture on a football card—any card. A good example is probably the TV

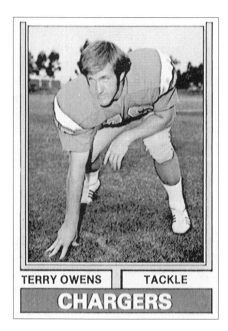

TERRY OWENS   TACKLE

CHARGERS

State Farm agent Terry Owens is not and never has been Hulk Hogan. *Pictured:* 1974 Topps Terry Owens #228.

Ed O'Neill, who went so far as to try out with the Steelers.

As it stands now, the glut of newer cards assures that many players who never would have been considered for a card in the old days are featured on one now. It took the football Ed O'Neil six years of slugging it out in the game to get his image on a common card in the 1970s. Today he probably would be on three or four in his first year alone. But commons have little appeal to the majority of collectors unless they are filling a set.

The newest hoax concerns another pair of commons, the two cards of former San Diego Charger tackle Terry Owens. The false rumor is that he later bloomed into superstar wrestler Hulk Hogan.

The Terry Owens rookie card is #284 in the Topps set of 1973, the first year Topps expanded to 528 cards. Another Owens card appears in the 1974 set, #228.

The truth is far more prosaic than the story. Today Owens is a successful State Farm agent based in Mobile, Alabama. He is not and never has been Hulk Hogan.

"Don't let anybody spend $20 on my account," Owens said modestly. "My card can't be worth much more'n 20 cents."

Owens' executive assistant, Green Suttles, says he has known Owens for 16 years, ever since Owens joined the agency.

"Terry is a big ol' teddy bear of a man," Green said. "We are very fond of him."

Plucked out of Jacksonville State in the 1966 draft, Terry Owens spent his entire NFL stint with the Chargers.

"My best year was definitely 1972, when I had good games against the Raiders and the Broncos," Owens said. "You know, we had to play those guys twice a year. It meant going up against Denver's Lyle Alzado and Ben Davidson of the Raiders."

Over the past year, Owens has been called many times by people eager to confirm the Hulk Hogan connection.

"It's just not true," he said. "I know who I am, and I'm not Hulk Hogan. I don't know how these things get started."

The kicker is that all the attention the hoaxes have generated has turned the O'Neil card and both Owens cards into collector's items. These cards are no longer quite so common as they once were.

Conjuring up card hoaxes seems to be the pastime of nameless unscrupulous people connected to the hobby. It is a cheap, shoddy racket, and collectors should not allow themselves to be taken in by such shenanigans.

But hoax or no hoax, collectors still compete to own the Ed O'Neil card and to a lesser extent those of Terry Owens. Before the hoax, the most glamorous thing about O'Neil's card was its proximity in number to the only card of authentic star Earl Campbell of the Houston Oilers, #390. Like the O'Neil card, the Terry Owens cards are regular commons. They should be worth perhaps a dollar in deluxe mint, which commonly they are not.

Today all the hoax cards are correctly listed in the guides as commons, usually worth between 10 and 25 cents, depending on grade. However, out on the street where the real prices are, they can cost far more.

Even if collectors know it ain't Al Bundy or the Hulkster.

ODDBALLS

In the oddball category, the football cards issued by Kahn's All Meat Wieners from 1959 to 1963 take first place. For serious collectors Kahn's are quality cards loaded with many desirable players. The original 1959 set featured players from the Cleveland Browns and the Pittsburgh Steelers. Both Bobby Layne and future Steelers coach Chuck Noll are included, Layne as a Steeler and Noll as a Brown.

What makes these truly oddball cards is the goofy slogan that every card carried: "Compliments of Kahn's—The Wiener the World Awaited."

Some of the largest football cards ever made were issued in 1970 by Clark Oil and Refining Corporation. These cards pictured players from eight separate NFL teams. Though designed by the artist Nicholas Volpe, they are not much as football cards and only get mentioned because of their huge (almost 8" by 10") size. Not until Action Packed released its limited edition "Mammoth" cards in late 1994 did cards approaching the Clark Volpe size appear.

The Laughlin Flaky Football set is one of the oddest. It's a rare 27-card joke set featuring cartoon teams with names like the Los Angeles Yams and New Orleans Scents. Copyrighted in 1975 by the artist R. G. Laughlin, it appeared at a time when the NFL had two fewer teams

Action Packed released the huge 7½″ by 10½″ "Mammoth" cards in late 1994. *Pictured:* 1994 Action Packed Mammoth Barry Sanders #MM3.

than it does now. Goodness knows what Laughlin would have done with the Seahawk and the Buccaneer names.

Rarely does the NFL allow itself to be teased anymore in the manner of the Laughlin set. The NFL is now a serious business. An example of this seriousness is the pompous music for NFL videos that often sounds like the score from the World War II documentary series *Victory at Sea.*

Topps put together an NFL set in 1977 geared for the Mexican market that fits in the oddball category.

According to Steve Galletta of Touchdown Cards in New York, Topps' south of the border series was done on the cheap. "The Mexican football cards have very thin cardboard and are made to be pulled apart by hand," Galletta said. "The one good feature is the wrappers—all four are quite colorful."

ERRORS

Error cards have dogged the hobby right from the beginning. The first error card was the Mayo Cut Plug card of Flying Wedge pioneer John William Dunlop, which appeared without his name. While today Dunlop's card can no longer be considered anonymous, it is still an error card.

The larger issue is how error cards are treated in the hobby. Some collectors seek errors, believing the value of the card is enhanced by some proofreading flub.

Others avoid them. They say an error devalues a card, since the company that issued it couldn't be bothered to have effective quality control. Frequent errors in a set mean bad

work was done, and bad work should mean a lower value.

One card in the legendary 1935 National Chicle set has three errors. On card #14, the card of Chicago Cardinal quarterback Phil Sarboe, his name is spelled Sorboe and his hometown is listed as Yokima, Washington.

Pardon me. That's *Sarboe* and the town is *Yakima.*

The Sarboe card also says Phil attended Washington University. Nobody in the Pacific Northwest calls the Seattle school Washington University. The Husky school is called many things, especially by Pacific-10 rivals, but never Washington University.

It's the *University of Washington.*

Error cards are dismayingly frequent in modern sets. Even glossy new sets like 1993 Pro Set Power

This one card in the legendary 1935 National Chicle set has three errors. *Pictured:* 1935 National Chicle Phil Sarboe #14.

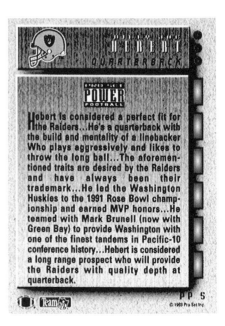

Errors are dismayingly frequent in modern sets, as evidenced in this 1993 Pro Set Power Billy Joe Hobert #PP5, front and reverse.

have glaring errors. Card #PP5 in Pro Set's Update Prospects subset misspells former Husky quarterback Billy Joe Hobert's last name as Hebert on the card back.

Fleer's 1990 football set, the company's first major football set in nearly 30 years, is riddled with errors. The most flagrant example is the Joe Montana error card, #10A. It mixes up his throwing yardage with his touchdown totals. Fleer substituted a corrected card later, #10B, but other errors remained in the set. In this set, errors and poor design made for a low-value product. A full three years after issue, this otherwise historic set sold for a pathetic $8.

Mistakes like the Montana error are inexcusable. Don't they have people who look at these cards be-

fore they print them? Isn't there any quality control? Card makers should consider hiring some football fans, who presumably would catch many of these goofs.

Fleer has made its share of mistakes, but leave it to Topps to produce the two worst and stupidest error cards of all time.

Yes, that's the famous Jim Taylor pair in the 1959 and 1960 Topps football sets.

The 1959 Topps set contains the rookie card of Green Bay Packer Jim Taylor. It is card #155. But the player pictured on the card is not the Green Bay fullback Jim Taylor, it is St. Louis Cardinal linebacker Jim Taylor.

You might think that it's not a big deal, a mistake is a mistake. It won't happen again. Topps will figure this one out.

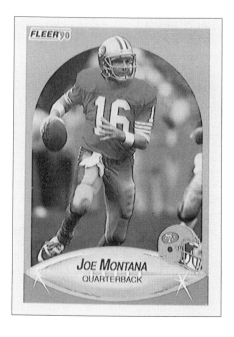

A gross example of an error card is Fleer's 1990 Joe Montana card. *Pictured, counterclockwise from top:* 1990 Fleer Joe Montana #10 front and #10A reverse and #10B reverse.

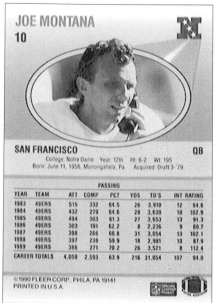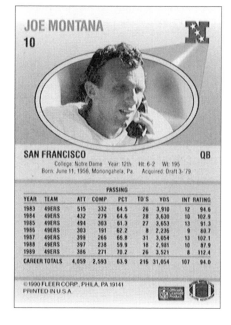

Wrong! In the 1960 Topps football set, the company made exactly the same mistake a second time! The back of card #52 lists the stats of Green Bay runner Jim Taylor, but the front again shows the face of Cardinal linebacker Jim Taylor.

Without a doubt, the Jim Taylor

Topps made the same Jim Taylor mistake again! *Pictured:* **1960 Topps Jim Taylor #52. The player shown is Cardinal linebacker Jim Taylor, not Packer fullback Jim Taylor.**

dual error cards are a feat that future card makers will be hard-pressed to surpass.

By the way, if you want to see what Green Bay's Jim Taylor actually looked like, check out Pacific's 1990 Packers 25th Anniversary set, #9. It has a nice photo of Lombardi's bruising fullback.

Collectors need to remember to be careful of facts. It's good to check when you're not sure. Don't just take somebody's word for something. If card makers regularly make flagrant mistakes, collectors are no less vulnerable.

Find out for yourself. Do research.

CHAPTER SIXTEEN

MINOR ISSUE FOOTBALL CARDS

Outside the Mainstream

Most of the football card sets produced since 1948 fall in the "minor issue" category. In fact, minor issue football card sets far outnumber mainstream issues.

The difference between minor issue cards and the nationally distributed mainstream sets is that minor issue cards are produced for collectors in a smaller geographical area. They are not generally known to the hobby at large until well after release.

Included in this category are police sets, food and candy sets, oversized cards, stamps, discs, coins, labels, stickers, and other novelty items. Most often these items are produced for a professional team by a regional sponsor, like a dairy or a soft drink bottler. Local sponsor cards are the rule rather than the exception in the minor issue part of the hobby.

For the sake of convenience, collectors classify things like discs, stamps, labels, and coins along with cards in the minor issue category. Unlike practical products such as hats, mugs, cups, and T-shirts, cards and similar items have no innate value. They can't really by used— just looked at.

Minor issues also tend to focus on individual teams or players, not football as a whole. And they do not appear in the popular price guides. When collector interest dictates an appearance, they aren't considered minor anymore.

National distribution alone doesn't guarantee major status for a football card set. The Swell series of professional football greats and the 1986 McDonald's cards enjoyed wide distribution but technically are considered minor issues. Low collector interest means a listing only in comprehensive card guides.

A common type of minor issue card is the police set. In large U.S. cities hosting pro football teams, agencies that advocate youth programs often distribute police set football cards to kids. A fairly typical example is the 1991 Police Sacramento Surge set, a 38-card WLAF set sponsored by American Airlines for People Reaching Out, a Sacramento counseling program. The Surge cards have color player photos on the fronts. The backs have biographical information and brief player quotes. The players in the Surge po-

#44 • John Riggins
Running Back
Washington Redskins

Police sets are noted for featuring positive messages geared to "at risk" youngsters. *Pictured:* 1983 Police Redskins John Riggins #15.

page from the police set book when they began issuing cards with inspirational messages in their mainstream products. Pro Set's 1991 Dan Marino card, for instance, is #726 in the "NFL Messages" subset. On the back Dan tells kids a better life begins in the classroom. The rest of the cards in the subset have similar messages. Clearly, police sets have influenced mainstream cards.

Another common message series is the "Smokey Bear" series, sponsored by NFL teams and the U.S. Forest Service to promote woodland safety. Smokey himself appears on every card, shovel in paw, to remind us to protect the forest. Though the majority of Smokey sets are not well-designed, a few are good. Two extremely attractive examples are the

lice set advise young people that success in life often depends on avoiding drug use and other negative behaviors. These are good cards with a strong message, but they have a low set value of $15.

Another good example of a police set is the 30-card "Birth of Pro Football" set issued in 1983 in Latrobe, Pennsylvania. Though they're not considered especially attractive, the Latrobe cards show many hardy pioneers of football, notably Cap Ryan, Doggie Trenchard, and John K. Brallier.

Companies like Pro Set took a

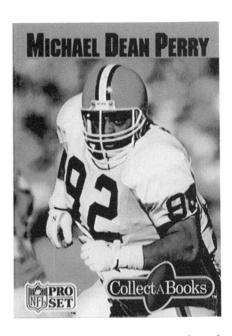

Pro Set CollectABooks became another minor issue keepsake. *Pictured:* 1990 Pro Set Michael Dean Perry CollectABook #34.

14-card 1988 Smokey Raiders and the 36-card 1988 Smokey Chargers.

Pro Set expanded on the standard card format to produce a 36-item set of CollectABooks in 1990. Featured in the series were CollectABooks for Eric Dickerson and Michael Dean Perry, who didn't rate football cards in Pro Set's regular 1990 release.

Food cards are another common type of minor issue. While mainstream cards have long been associated with chewing gum, minor issue cards represent an entire snack array.

A fast-food hamburger stand in South Florida issued the 1967 Royal Castle Dolphin cards, a set featuring Bob Griese in his rookie year. That card, #10 in the set, is no doubt worth the $250 it commands in near-mint

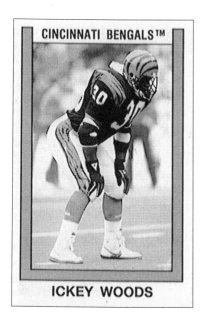

CINCINNATI BENGALS™

ICKEY WOODS

Cards issued by food establishments (food cards) are a mainstay of minor issue football sets. *Pictured:* 1989 Panini Ickey Woods #234.

condition. Rarely is a minor issue card so valuable.

In 1988 Panini Stickers appeared. They had been made for years prior to 1988 under Topps' license. In the first year alone, sandwich grill maker Panini produced 457 different stickers. Not one of them has ever cost more than a dollar.

The 1962–63 Salada Tea football coins are an exceptional series, depicting players from both the AFL and the NFL before the merger. A complete 154-piece set could probably fetch $2,000.

Over in convenience-store land, the 7-Eleven chain brought out a pair of plastic coin sets in 1983 and 1984. The main selling point was an alternating action and portrait photo of the player. 7-Eleven's 1983 set had only 15 coins, including Raider Marcus Allen and 49er Joe Montana. The 1984 set was larger, at 40 coins. Together, they might cost a collector around $70.

A new descendant of the coin is the popular POG. These circular cardboard collectibles appear to have originated in Hawaii. There the round things served as stoppers for passion, orange, and guava drink, a favored local beverage sold in glass bottles.

The POG is popular because it is used in a stacking game where POGs are turned over with a POGlike plastic slammer. The first to turn over six POGs in a stack of 11 wins.

There seems to be an almost endless variety of minor issue football items. A couple of excellent Canadian Football League coin sets were released by Nalley's in 1963 and 1964. The coins could be mounted on

POGs are both game pieces and collectibles. *Pictured, from left to right:* **Dallas Cowboys POG and Los Angeles Raiders POG.**

nifty little plastic shields, each designed for a different CFL team. Shields were made for five CFL clubs in 1964—the B.C. Lions, the Calgary Stampeders, the Edmonton Drillers, the Saskatchewan Shockers, and the Winnipeg Blue Bombers.

More CFL minor issues worth mentioning are the Saskatchewan and Ottawa police sets released in the early 1980s. The card fronts feature color action photos of CFL players, and on the backs are brief biographies and safety tips. Printed in gorgeous color, these CFL cards are extremely well-done and represent the best of what minor football issues are all about.

Back in the United States, winning first prize for most attractive minor issue set is the 1982 Police Miami Dolphins set, a 16-card wonder displaying Shula's crew in their pre–Dan Marino days. The clean, balanced design, sharp logos, and superb use of four-color ink separations made for a product second to none.

Why do companies issue minor football card sets? They want some

of the excitement of professional sport to rub off on themselves. Handled properly, giveaways and promotions can boost the sales of products, as parents of small children know all too well. But you have to wonder how many extra gallons of gas Sunoco sold because collectors wanted Sunoco's 1972 NFL album and stamp set. Let's hope it was a lot, because the 624-item stamp set offers a richly detailed look at the NFL that year.

You also might wonder what benefit Knudsen's Dairy got from its 1989 and 1990 Raider, Charger, and 49er bookmark sets, designed to promote youth reading and literacy. Probably Knudsen's Dairy got little corporate benefit from the bookmark promotion, but it was a nice gesture.

Wilkes-Barre, Pennsylvania, card dealer Joe Sak says his customers value the complete minor issue football sets he sells. "There's a small but growing market for minor football," Sak said. "My 1982 Carrollton Park Mall Cowboys set sells well, as does my 100-card set of LSU Tiger greats."

In the minor issue category, sets

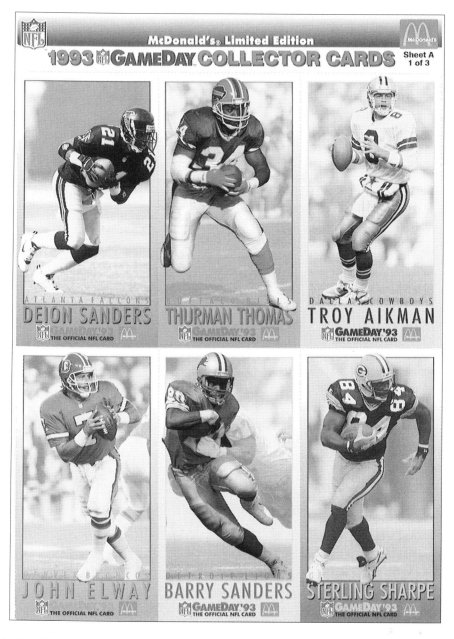

McDonald's special 1993 NFL GameDay sets were the minor issue highlight of the season. *Pictured:* 1993 McDonald's/GameDay Collector cards, Sheet A.

often focus on individual teams or players from a single school. Sometimes they zero in on college players or showcase a college league.

"I have a 1983 Cramer Legends set of great Pacific-10 players I consider a good value," Sak added. "It has O. J. Simpson and Ernie Nevers in it, among others. Another good seller is my 1976 Crane disc set, which is notable for its Walter Payton rookie."

National interest in football cards can be measured by minor issue releases like McDonald's 1993 distribution of NFL GameDay cards at its restaurants. This was the minor issue highlight of the season. Brilliantly colored and superbly done by Fleer/GameDay, the McDonald's cards are a collector's delight. They were also a good value at just $1 for a three-sheet set of 18 cards.

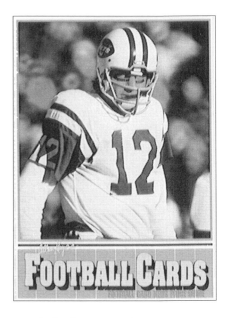

A particular focus on a player was once the province of minor issue cards. *Pictured:* 1990 Football Card News Joe Namath #1.

Minor issue cards are now getting swamped by the mass of major football card issues. As Topps dominance faded in the national market, even local heroes became fair game for the major card companies. Fleer distributed a 1992 Mark Rypien set that shouldn't have much appeal beyond the Washington Beltway, and Pacific issued a 1992 nine-card Steve Largent subset for this former Seahawk great. A particular focus on a player or team was once strictly the province of the minor issue. No longer.

In a market as fluid as the football card hobby, the crowd races to whatever happens to be the latest thing. The latest thing changes every few months, but such is the nature of football cards. In the minor issue category, the pace has been accelerated by what is happening in the main-

stream part of the hobby. Competition among mainstream companies like Fleer, Score, Pro Set, Action Packed, and Topps now runs hot and heavy.

The successful minor issue card must have a player focus that sells it, like the first-year card of a star like Walter Payton or Bob Griese. The alternative is to invent an angle everybody else has missed. Either task is difficult.

So where does this leave us as collectors? Opportunities still exist for well-executed minor issue cards. Police sets will remain strong, with recognized sets for most major NFL teams.

Local sponsors committed to a team or people with a good idea to sell won't be deterred by overproduction of mainstream cards. Minor

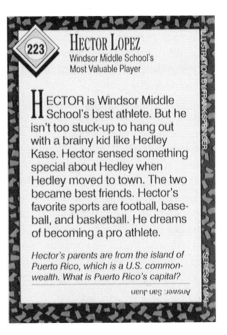

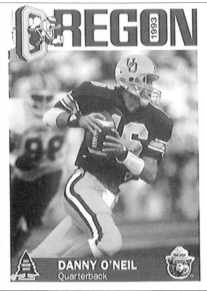

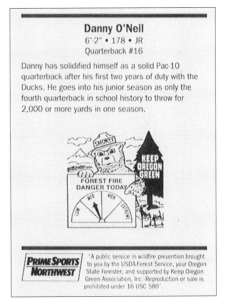

Positive messages have always been the strong suit of minor issue football cards. *Pictured, from top:* 1994 Sports Illustrated for Kids Hector Lopez #223 front and reverse and 1993 Smokey Danny O'Neil front and reverse.

issue card makers have good reasons for making minor cards and will probably continue. For them collectors are only an afterthought, not the main reason for being.

Distributing a product featuring positive messages has been the strong suit of minor issues. A good minor issue football card can spur an interest in sports among disadvantaged or troubled young people. Minor issue cards like police sets tell young people that recognition can come from excellence in sports and other things. Police set minor issue cards have traditionally cornered the market on uplifting messages. They will likely retain that distinction in the future.

For football players, appearing on a football card—even a minor issue card—is proof of success. Once the game is over and playing days are just a memory, there is always the card, perhaps even more than one, to bring back years spent in the sport.

The wide variety of minor issue football cards makes them sometimes difficult to classify, but they are always intriguing. And at least some great minor issue cards are still unknown to the hobby, just waiting to be discovered by intrepid collectors. In the meantime, minor issue cards, though rarely valuable, offer an interesting sideline for collectors stale on mainstream material.

THE HOBBY OF COLLECTING

CHAPTER SEVENTEEN

SMALL-BUDGET FOOTBALL CARD COLLECTING

Smart Purchases Pay Big Dividends

COLLECT SMART

Trading card hobbyists define the small-budget football card collector as someone who spends an average of $10 to $15 per month on cards. Because of the explosion in product, the small-budget collector faces a large problem: so many cards and so little money. Good material abounds. It's too much of a good thing—not every choice goodie can get the full focus of your attention.

But savvy football card collectors on a budget can narrow the field of desirable cards without missing any fun. The main thing to remember is that while the investment aspect of your collection is appealing, the real reason you collect is that you enjoy it. Those little slips of cardboard featuring gridiron gladiators are neat to look at, contain interesting data, and often have historical value. Modern-era football cards are especially good. Still, at the end, collectors don't want to be saddled with good cards of low or marginal value. Collectors want to exercise care in their choices.

Faced with a purchase, buyers in other hobbies invoke the three basic questions of collectibility. Number

one asks: Does everyone sell this? If the answer is yes, it's not a scarce item but a commonplace item. Number two asks: Is everyone after this right now? If the second answer is yes, it's probably going to cost more than you'll ever get from it, at least in the short term. Number three is the tough one: Will everyone want this

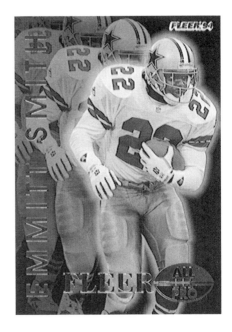

Is everyone after this card right now? *Pictured:* **1994 Fleer All Pro Emmitt Smith #17.**

someday? If the third answer is yes, you might have something worth a second look.

Scarcity is not the only measure by which card values are determined. It is, however, an important one. Are you making most of your purchases at discount stores or other national retail outfits? Few cards bought this way are likely to be scarce. And if they're not scarce, they have a strike against them as far as collectors are concerned. A safer bet is finding cards at shows, hobby stores, or through direct mail via magazines. These outlets are better sources of the more exotic products, like old cards, rookie sets, cards from Brand X football leagues, updates, and short print factory sets. Odd and

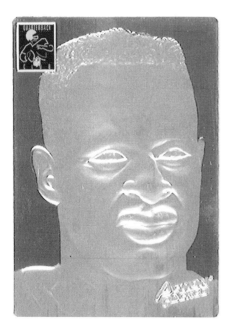

The value of odd and offbeat products such as this 1994 Action Packed Jerry Rice QB7 usually rises faster than that of overproduced mainline stuff.

offbeat products usually rise faster than overproduced mainline stuff. It takes extra effort to track down special cards and sets, but the energy spent can be very worthwhile.

Consider the Score 1989 football factory set, for example. As recently as April 1990, this set sold for about $35. Practically all the sets sold went through hobby outlets. Now it's selling for $150 to $220. Mass retailers never saw this product.

Football cards in general are attractive, but collectors especially love those that have the capacity to move on the hobby market. Opportunities exist for collectors who have an eye for value, style, and the special qualities that make an item great. The main reasons for the advance of the 1989 Score set are obvious in retrospect: scarcity and quality. It was a little hard to find and the best, most comprehensive set around, superior to both the competing Topps and Pro Set products available that year.

Another solid approach is advocated by West Coast dealer Dennis Hooker, owner of Hooker's Sports Cards & Collectibles. He advocates finding rookie and early cards of upper-level players from the 1970s through the mid-1980s.

"As a dealer I often see Topps football collections loaded with quality players whose card values haven't started moving," Hooker says. "By that I mean players like former Jet Rich Caster or the rookie cards of guys like Raider Howie Long, quarterback Neil Lomax, Mel Gray, Kellen Winslow, Terry Metcalf, Rocky Bleier. . . . There are a lot of them. Many of these cards can be had for

Many football card collections contain quality players whose card values haven't risen yet. This 1972 Topps Richard Caster #68 is one example.

less than five bucks, sometimes as little as one or two. Check out prices for equivalent players in the 1960–65 period, and you can figure the potential."

Hooker also says that even though Topps cards of the 1970s to the mid-1980s are still relatively common, they're well past issue and could get hot as the hobby grows.

"I'm not saying that every one of these cards is a winner," Hooker adds. "I'm simply saying that my experience tells me that this is where price rises are coming due."

No one can absolutely know which cards will fly and which will languish year after year. It's a gamble. But a card or card set you don't see sold at the supermarket has advantages. If there's some special touch pulling it out of the ordinary, you have something to gamble on. When you develop the ability to spot cards that will move up, you have taken a giant stride toward making big profits on a small budget.

PICK TEN

Another way collectors on a budget can get a bigger bang for their hobby dollar is to seek out specific player cards rather than entire sets.

Although the football card market today is glutted with releases, significant material can be found even in ordinary sets. That's because nobody really knows in advance which players have the necessary drive and durability to make it as superstars. As a consequence, many recent-vintage football cards appear to have strong investment potential.

The new hot players may change every season, but those collectors who like to make small gambles on the careers of football players find it irresistible to try to predict the future.

There are some recent football cards that have made dramatic upward moves. For these cards, the future is now. Two that come to mind are the 1989 Action Packed Mark Rypien card and the 1990 Fleer Update Emmitt Smith card. In early 1991 the Rypien card was going for about $2.50. One Super Bowl later, Rypien's card was listed in the guides at $20.00.

As of January 1991, the 1990 Fleer Update set was selling for $19.00 or less. But today, with the fortunes of both Emmitt Smith and the Dallas Cowboys on the rise, buying the Fleer Update set for under $40.00 requires hard bargaining. More than half the value of the Fleer Update set comes from Smith's card, the first major issue for this talented back. Should America's Team make it to the Super Bowl once or twice more during Smith's career, watch out! The Fleer Update Smith card could zoom higher than the 1986 Topps Jerry Rice rookie.

Remember too that light production and limited availability of both sets enhanced the value of these cards. In the case of Rypien, the premium quality of the Action Packed card pushes it up as well.

How do we identify other cards with this kind of investment potential? Three conditions ought to apply: 1) They should be rookie or draft pick cards; 2) The cards should still be fairly cheap on the hobby market; and 3) They must be easy to obtain in quantity—five or six, maybe even a dozen.

We should also recognize that most collectors are after that star offensive player. When was the last time collectors got really excited about a safety or a noseguard? Only rarely are linemen or defenders

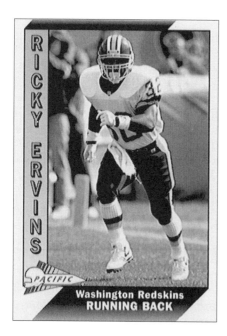

Significant material can be found even in ordinary sets. *Pictured:* the rookie 1991 Pacific Ricky Ervins #659.

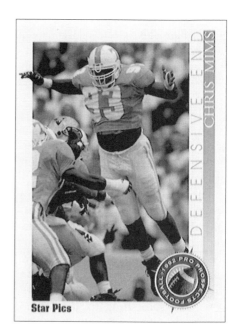

Investment cards should be fairly cheap on the hobby market. *Pictured:* the draft 1992 Star Pics Chris Mims #92.

found on a really hot card. What collectors want most are quarterbacks, running backs, and a few outstanding receivers.

Choosing from among the many rookie cards on the market is tricky. Still, if you methodically examine recent releases, you'll find some possible movers on nearly every roster. A little bit of careful thought narrows the list down to ten.

It should be remembered that this is strictly guesswork, and it's likely that some guesses, if not all, are wrong. Football card collectors have displayed some pretty quicksilver tendencies over the years. What they pick up, they can also drop, sometimes in short order. The once hot but now refrigerator-cold William Perry

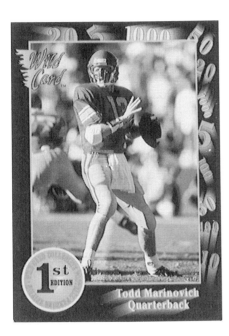

Wild Card brought out an attractive card for rifle-armed rookie Todd Marinovich. *Pictured:* **1991 Wild Card Draft Picks Todd Marinovich #35.**

error card is a prime example. As far as the accuracy of these choices goes—well, let the hobbyist be the judge.

1. Todd Marinovich—1991 Wild Card NFL, #147. Tempermental Todd has lessons to learn but could again become an NFL-caliber quarterback. Marinovich's 1994 move to the more wide-open CFL was probably a good thing for his development.

Wild Card brought out a very attractive rookie card for this left-hander who boasts an arm like a whip. Take the long view and remember how well Marinovich can play. What he did for USC might happen in the CFL too. Also look for a numbered stripe on the front to give the card greater value. Wild Card's gimmick of giving collectors a chance to trade in their stripes for more cards was a clever one.

2. Johnnie Morton—1994 Fleer Ultra First Rounder, #14. Here's another USC product with talent to burn. Morton is a fleet, gutty receiver who routinely makes the miracle catch. He finally got a chance to play late in the 1994 season and right away delivered for his team. The premium quality of the Fleer card gives it extra oomph without going overboard. A bargain at $2.00.

3. William Floyd—1994 Classic Pro Line, #355. This hot 49er fullback has awesome potential and high visibility on a glamour team. At less than a dollar, this card is practically a steal.

4. J. J. Birden—1991 Score 90 Plus player subset, #326. The Chiefs' speedy receiver has Anthony Carter–style moves and displays exceptional courage on crossing routes. In a crucial 1991 game, Birden single-

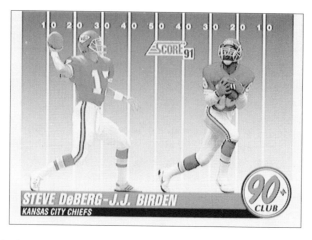

J. J. Birden and other Kansas City receivers benefited from Joe Montana's presence. *Pictured:* 1991 Score J. J. Birden #326.

handedly broke open a close contest with two long scoring catches.

Football legend Joe Montana's service with the Chiefs helped advance Birden's long-range prospects. The only thing Birden and other Kansas City receivers lacked was someone who could get them the ball.

5. Chris Zorich—1991 Fleer Ultra, #298. Here's an exception to the rule that collectors only want star offensive players. This Chicago Bear defensive tackle is the latest definitive "Monster of the Midway." The card will have more luster in the future because it is part of Fleer's first entry into the high-end market.

6. Heath Shuler—1994 Game-Day, #414. Expect Washington coach Norval Turner to quickly exploit this quarterback's long-ball ability. Once that happens, fans can expect the Redskins to begin the long trek back to the Super Bowl. Unfortunately, GameDay has chosen to join the chase card craze with four ritzy 1994 subsets. Ignore them and chase this regular rookie showing Shuler in pro uniform.

7. Alvin Harper—1991 Score II, #589. Tall and athletic, this Dallas receiver evokes memories of Drew Pearson. The 1991 Score II series earned distinction by offering a wealth of rookies who nabbed starting spots on their respective clubs. A low initial cost of 60 cents for this card augurs well for a future payoff.

8. Desmond Howard—1992 Classic, #1 or LP1. Rookie cards showing the player in pro uniform usually have more allure than draft pick cards, but Howard's draft card carries the weight of his Heisman Trophy and the instant recognition he received in Washington (which until recently was one of the NFL's most consistent teams). The 1992 Classic set featured ten limited production (LP) foil stamped cards. Only 40,000 total were made. No doubt the Howard LP1 card will be, in the long run, the more coveted of the two first cards.

9. Scott Mitchell—1992 Wild Card World League, #67. Miami seasoned this backup to Dan Marino in the World League, where he performed way above expectations. A big, strong player who can throw a touch pass as well as a bullet, Mitchell beat out Kerwin Bell for the Orlando Thunder starting job. Wild Card was right to include this potential great in its World League set.

10. Raghib Ismail—1991 All World CFL, #92. When the Rocket Raghib lands in the United States, this card could be on par with Joe Theismann's 1971 OPC card. All World went overboard by including eight other Rocket cards in its 110-card set, but who can blame them? As Coach Paul Brown used to say

Heisman Trophy winners like Desmond Howard have instant allure for card collectors. *Pictured:* 1992 Classic Desmond Howard #1.

The Score series laid it on thick with rookies like Alvin Harper, who have big-time potential. *Pictured:* 1991 Score Alvin Harper #589.

about his star running back, Jim Brown, "When you've got a big gun, you go ahead and shoot it."

The idea behind this exercise is to see if you can beat the crowd rather than just follow along, as many collectors seem to do. Applying the football knowledge you have accumulated over the years can help direct your choice of cards to collect.

Ask yourself: Do you want to pay top dollar or do you want to get paid top dollar? The ten cards mentioned above are just a few possibilities from among the cards of many players waiting for their chance in the big show. Card collectors who know football also know there are plenty of others as well.

CHAPTER EIGHTEEN

THE ART OF SELLING FOOTBALL CARDS

A Conversation with Dave Kelts, Card Shop Owner

This is how it is to be a card shop owner.

"We got a call from Hiron's—you know, the drug and variety store here in town," Dave Kelts said. "They told us somebody had broken in and made off with several cases of sports cards. They asked us to be on the lookout. Sure enough, he showed up here."

Kelts looked around the interior of Eugene Sports Cards on Blair Boulevard in Eugene, Oregon. "He had the very stuff Hiron's told us about. I bought a couple boxes he brought in, insisting on paying him by check. He didn't like it, but he took the check. The police got the information they needed from the bank when he cashed it and arrested him. Turns out he has multiple burglary convictions, all from card shops."

"You mean this was a criminal who specialized in stealing sports cards?" I asked.

"That's right."

Dave Kelts seemed pleased with his role in apprehending the most dreaded creature card shop owners must face. Kelts pointed to the sign above his Polaroid camera, which says he reserves the right to photograph sellers during transactions.

"It's a warning to thieves, nothing more," he said. "I've never had to use it."

Mostly Dave Kelts simply avoids questionable transactions.

"Eventually, as a dealer, you get a feel for what's right and what isn't right. Once a guy came in and dumped a large box of cards on my counter. He said he didn't want them and I could have them. I tried to get him to hang around so we could appraise them. Appraisals and putting together full sets are my specialties. But he just left. A few days later, he came back with even more cards. Finally I talked him into accepting an offer."

Dave Kelts pushed his wheelchair away from his worktable.

"The reason most of us get involved in card collecting is that it's fun," he said, rolling up his sleeves. As one of about 50,000 card shop owners in the United States, Dave Kelts does most of his business at the street level, handling customers who come in through the door.

Smiling, Kelts added: "I got involved in the card hobby as an adult myself, following my interest in baseball players like Tim McCarver and Roberto Clemente. The guys I admire the most in any sport are the ones who are successful and get ahead while conducting themselves with class."

By all accounts Dave Kelts fits that description as well. A successful card shop owner since 1985, he is frank about the current state of the football card hobby.

"The oversupply of football card sets is so bad that few collectors even know how many different brands there are. You can't run a predictable business when the collectors are so bewildered."

Football cards have grown from a hobby that few were interested in a decade ago to a glamour sector in a phenomenal new trading card industry. Unfortunately for many, the sheer number of football issues and the market preference for premium product has thrown a large monkey wrench in the works.

"Dealers are confused because collectors are confused. You can't go out on a limb with football products today. Take the 1990 Score factory set, for instance. Remember, the one that came in the red box? It was a loser for anybody who touched it. The 1989 Score set had sold so fast that the company thought they could do no wrong. They overprinted the 1990 set, and a lot of people lost money. I'm selling the ones I have left at $10 each."

Asked what he thinks about the future of football cards, Kelts shook his head.

"I see a big shakeout coming—not

A lot of people lost money on 1990 Score cards. *Pictured:* 1990 Score Andre Ware #607.

just in the number of shops around but among the manufacturers as well. I'm not sure we'll see more than half a dozen football sets five years from now. At least it won't be like it is today, with 20 different major 1992 football sets listed in the guides, not counting the World League, CFL, Classic cards, and promotions."

"How good are the price guides?"

Kelts grew thoughtful. "Pretty good. Beckett's guide seems to be the rule out here in the West. Other guides hold more sway back East. Some guides do well by zeroing in on the movers in different card sets, either up or down, rather than trying to do a little of everything, as Beckett's does."

Dave Kelts grew up in Lakeview,

Oregon, a place so small there weren't many cards around, much less collectors.

"Like I said, I came to the hobby as an adult. When I went into business in 1985, football card collecting ranked a distant second to baseball. Now it's more like a close second. No doubt baseball will always be first because it has a strong collector base and a long history, but football will stay close."

An automobile accident put Kelts in a wheelchair as a young adult.

"The shop is just hanging on right now, basically paying its own expenses but not much more. Until the competition subsides somewhat, it'll be tough to eke out more than a small profit. I see my role as going the extra distance for my customers, sending out a newsletter, and having a knack for filling sets."

Despite the uneasy state of the football card hobby, Kelts is generally optimistic about the future and pleased when he is able to make a difference.

"Score set up a promotion for dealers at Super Bowl XXV, and we were one of the winners. Franco Harris was the host that year, and we had a fine time. Later on I had a chance to give input on Score's selection of players for its 1991 set. I used the opportunity to tell them about Bill Musgrave, the University of Oregon quarterback sensation who broke the collegiate passing records of Dan Fouts and Chris Miller. Sure

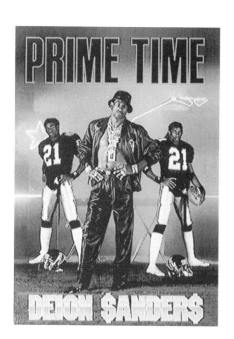

Football card collecting now runs a close second to baseball card collecting. *Pictured:* 1992 PrimeTime Deion Sanders #161.

Sure enough, Bill Musgrave appeared in the 1991 Score set as #569. *Pictured:* 1991 Score Bill Musgrave #569.

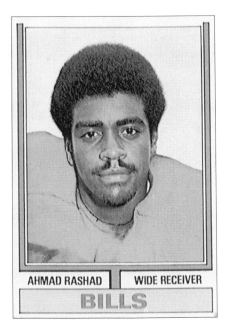 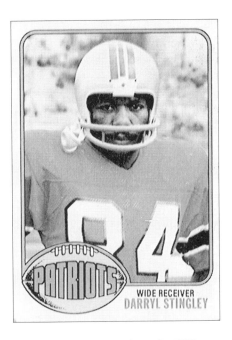

From an investment standpoint, the best bet now is older cards—those from the 1970s and earlier. *Pictured, from left to right:* **1974 Topps Ahmad Rashad #105** and **1976 Topps Darryl Stingley #324.**

enough, Musgrave appeared in the 1991 Score set as card #569."

"You don't have to sell me on Bill Musgrave," I answered. "Not one of his passes in the 1992 preseason fell incomplete. It was the perfect preseason. He's going to be another Fouts or Van Brocklin, if he ever gets a chance to play."

"As smart a player as there is in the game today," Kelts mused. "He's someone the 49ers are hiding from the league. Let's hope someday he gets a chance to start."

Dave Kelts smiled again and said: "Of course, from an investment standpoint the best bet now is older cards, items from the 1970s and before. With a volatile market like the one we have today, it's just possible the older cards will come through. With the old cards,

you know where you stand. The same isn't true of the new cards, however nice they may be."

For Kelts one of the advantages of being a dealer with an everyday card business is that it keeps him informed.

Operating from his store as a full-service dealer, Kelts has to know about all aspects of the card business. In his regular newsletter, Kelts was one of the first to notice the sudden paucity of 1993 NBA basketball cards: "A genuine scarcity of basketball cards has driven the prices of cases, boxes, and packs through the roof," Kelts wrote. "Evidence seems to show that production quantities are down across the board, while demand is increasing. The prices we are now seeing are a true reflection of demand. A prevailing climate among the card companies to keep production at reasonable levels is having a powerful impact on prices."

In other issues of his regular newsletter, Kelts has reported on subjects as varied as the demise of the Star Pics company, major league baseball's court fight with *Ball Street Journal,* and the advanced photo qualities of newer cards. He also shares his acumen by reviewing recent products like Fleer Ultra, Pinnacle, and Upper Deck baseball.

Here's a typical example: "The 1993 Fleer Ultra Baseball Series I issue reached us recently, and we found the basic set all too similar to their 1992 issue. This similarity problem was also the case with Score's 1993 Pinnacle set. Changes were

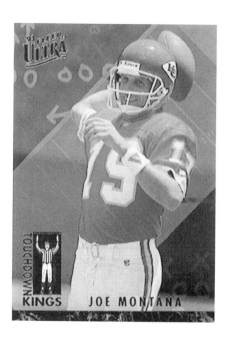

Being in on the start of something hot is what makes this hobby fun. *Pictured:* 1993 Fleer Ultra Joe Montana TDK #4.

made in the logo on the front and the photos on the back, but there is still little difference between the 1992 and 1993 cards.

"We were, however, pleased to find that we could get a full set of the first series out of a box. While the card designs did not change much from last year, the Award Winners insert set did change quite noticeably. For example, the design of the Gold Glove winners differs substantially from the Cy Young and MVP awards."

To stay in business as a dealer, Dave Kelts must be well-versed in the details of all the major sports sets—football, basketball, and baseball. These days, however, it is the great basketball card shortage of 1993 that has him vexed.

I asked why the card companies would hold down production on an item that obviously makes money for them.

"The NBA denies forcing the card companies to hold down production," he answered. "But while the NBA is not controlling production levels, they are clearly interested in seeing that NBA-licensed companies are not overproducing products in a way that might hurt the image of the NBA."

It's always something. Either the companies are putting collectors off by making too many cards or frustrating them by making too few. A happy medium is not easily reached.

"As both a collector and a shop owner, what motivates you the most?" I asked.

"Being in on the start of something hot. It's the thing that makes this hobby fun."

CHAPTER NINETEEN

FOOTBALL CARD PERIPHERALS

Beyond the Shoebox

In most cases, it's not enough anymore to simply collect football cards and stash them away in an old shoebox. Hundreds and even thousands of cards might be easy to square away, but when a collection starts to run into the tens of thousands, storage can become a bulky problem. Collectors now have dozens of new ways to package the cards they own, thanks to the twin sciences of preservation and storage.

The importance of preservation cannot be overstated. To make cards last as long as possible, collectors must take care to keep them safe, dry, free of dust, and protected from sunlight. The use of acid-free paper and non-oxidizing plastic in preservation will help keep valuable cards fresh well into the next century. Even a small investment in card preservation material makes good sense because the cards will hold a higher grade for a longer time.

High-grade cards command premium prices at resale time. And sooner or later, every collection must be resold.

Good storage emphasizes convenience and uses minimal space. All

The importance of card preservation cannot be overstated. *Pictured:* 1994 Game-Day Dan Wilkinson #74.

collectors want to be able to admire their cards without having to go through a lot of difficult finding and sorting. Collectors also want to confine their cards in the smallest possible physical area to reduce space conflicts with other family members.

Many products are now available to help collectors who want to keep their precious football cards in top condition. These products can also be used for baseball, hockey, basketball, and other standard-sized trading cards. But here the discussion concerns football only.

In addition to the obvious hobby supplies like storage boxes, display cases, and plastic sleeves, there are hobby services ranging from buyer's clubs to authentication and grading consultants. For the electronically inclined, there are also sophisticated computer programs to help hobbyists track collections.

The first line of protection is the soft plastic sleeve. It's usually made of card-safe polypropylene. Plastic sleeves are often the initial purchase of collectors who have exited from the junior ranks to the investment side of the football hobby. At the very least, a clear plastic sleeve saves your most desirable cards from the wear caused by the oil and dirt always present on human hands.

A step up from this is the top loader, the most popular plastic storage case. It's a semirigid clear plastic sleeve used most often by dealers to display their more costly wares. Top

Good storage emphasizes convenience and uses minimal space. *Pictured:* 1992 SkyBox PrimeTime Jerry Rice #00A.

Tracking thousands of cards is a major task for collectors. *Pictured:* 1975 Topps Joe Gilliam #182.

146

loaders are usually used by dealers in card shop display cases or at shows. Some top loaders have the words "rookie card" embossed on them. The best top loaders are big enough to allow the card to fit in a soft plastic sleeve as well, thus affording extra protection.

Next we can look at the old shoebox, which today is a shoebox in name only.

Sue Bockenstette of Bock's Old Shoeboxes Inc. offers a wooden card box fitted with interior dividers and a closing hasp. The Bock's box comes in many sizes, is felt-lined, and features a brass nameplate that can be engraved with up to three letters.

"My husband, Patrick, came up with the idea after he discovered his old baseball cards in a shoebox at his parents' home," Sue Bockenstette said. "Damp conditions had left them in very poor shape."

The "Hall of Fame" box marketed by the Bockenstettes is their best seller, having a capacity of 1,550 cards or 750 if mounted in plastic top loaders.

A card collection in a Bockenstette box would probably wash ashore in perfect condition even if it fell overboard while you were on your annual sea cruise.

However, wooden boxes are for those special sets deserving of first cabin accommodations. A more ordinary batch of cards is likely to be housed in cardboard.

Cardboard storage boxes should be made from acid-free paper and be sturdy yet flexible. The best are double-walled to ensure strength and shock resistance. Fortunately for collectors, a huge selection of cardboard storage options is now available. The wide variety means that there are storage solutions for collections of every size.

Baseball Card World boxes are some fairly typical examples. Mammoth numbers of cards may be put away in Baseball Card World's Monster and Super Monster boxes. In the old days, it took a pretty dedicated collector to amass the 3,200 cards required to fill a Monster Box. And anybody who managed to sock away the 5,000 cards it takes to fill BCW's Super Monster Box before 1970 is now either a successful dealer or a millionaire or both.

Another interesting item is the BCW vault box, which will hold up to 500 cards in top loaders. Collectors can be assured that the cards are safe in a low-cost, sturdy box.

Ten Monster or ten Super Monster boxes cost $25, a small price to pay for a complete storage solution. If a collection is edging into the high numbers (more than around 10,000 cards), a small investment in storage can pay big dividends down the line. Not only do storage boxes keep a card collection in a dry and safe environment, but they also assure easy access.

The Card House is a 12-section box with a dozen individual drawers. These are often purchased by dealers to assemble common cards conveniently. Customers may then riffle through the drawers of a Card House for those needed set fillers. Almost 10,000 cards can be deployed in a Card House, and it is a must for retail card vendors who have to set up quickly.

Plastic cases come in an almost infinite variety. Clear plastic generic cases holding one, five, ten, 15, 25, 30, 35, 50, 100, 150, and 200 cards are sold at conventions, shows, shops, and through the mail for fairly reasonable prices—usually about $1 for the large size and 50 cents for the small.

Card albums are another neat device for showing off that grouping of extra-special cards.

The nine-card plastic pocket page makes card albums attractive. The page has holes to fit into a three-ring binder. Pages with fewer pockets are also available, like the six-pocket page designed to hold odd-sized cards like the Topps 1965 football set.

Slightly oversized pocket pages able to accommodate 1950s-era cards like the 1955 Topps All-American set are also being marketed to collectors who require the right tool for the job. Album books are nearly always traditional three-ring binders, sometimes with football-style artwork on the cover.

Once you've mastered the business of storing and preserving your collection, there remains the task of tracking many thousands of accumulated cards. How do you know what you have?

More than a dozen computer programs are being sold to help people track extensive card collections electronically. All computer trading card programs are essentially database programs. They provide a ready-made form collectors can see on screen. The form has spaces on it where collectors can write in information—like the name of the player, the year of the card, the company that issued the card, grade, defects, price, and so forth. Once input, the data can be manipulated, usually to see what a collection is worth. The most sophisticated of these programs come with much of the grunt work already done.

The Sports Card Manager is a

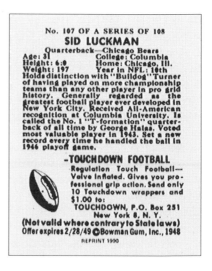

Collectors can list player, year, and card manufacturer on sophisticated databases. *Pictured:* 1948 Bowman Sid Luckman #107 front and reverse.

typical example of a trading card computer program. It features pull-down menus, special search commands, convenient price updating, and printing capabilities for many different types of reports. The program can also track more than one collection, so that it can follow football, baseball, basketball, nonsports, and any other trading card collection with equal facility. By mail Sports Card Manager retails for slightly over $40.

Two drawbacks to Sports Card Manager are that it requires at least a hard disk to operate and exists only in MS-DOS format.

Ballcards is made by the Bob-Kit Software Company of Detroit. It has most of the same features found in Sports Card Manager, but they are arranged in a much different style. Collectors who try Ballcards seem to end up swearing by it, and Bob-Kit offers a special evaluation copy of the program to interested collectors. Built-in data is available for different sports in Ballcards. My evaluation copy of the program had only the 1992 Series I Wild Card football set included.

Ballcards requires a hard drive but is nonetheless easy to install. Simple commands tell files in the program to expand on disk, much as you might inflate an air mattress. An attractive opening screen allows the user to sift through program options with little trouble. Ballcards has pull-down menus, excellent graphics, and a mass edit function that allows quick updates of many cards at once.

Sports Nuts of Fort Walton Beach, Florida, makes a program called Card Nuts designed to be easy to use. It can track more than one type of collection and works well on older equipment, like computers without hard disks, as well as computers that have hard disks.

Sports Nuts offers Card Nuts software at a relatively modest price of only $24.95 postpaid.

Even less expensive than Card Nuts is the program offered by the MCR company of Fort Collins, Colorado. Selling for a mere $19.95 retail, MCR's program is called Card Management System. It is also available for Windows at $24.95. Like the others, Card Management System tracks any card type, features pull-down menus, and can produce printed reports.

The basic $19.95 Card Management System will work on any computer with at least 512K RAM and dual 360K floppy disk drives.

MCR owner Mike Yoder says his basic program nevertheless holds a large amount of data. "Card Management System can track 8,000 to 10,000 entries," Yoder said, "depending on how much detail is included."

Most of the computer programs available to aid card collectors are written in the MS-DOS format. One exception is Ablesoft's The Card Collector. Available in both the Apple Macintosh format and MS-DOS, The Card Collector comes in versions for football, baseball, and hockey. The football version lists cards from more than 50 sets, from 1948 through 1993. It allows collectors to tag cards in any one of three conditions. The advantage to having the sets prelisted on the program is that collectors can go through the program checking off their own cards without having to

Monthly updates of card prices may be obtained from computer software makers. *Pictured:* 1994 Fleer Ultra First Rounder Johnnie Morton #14.

enter a lot of data. Simply look, check, and mark. That's all there is to it. Then you can have the computer tell you the value of what you've marked.

You can get monthly updates of card values from Ablesoft so your prices can be regularly brought up-to-date. If your collection is extensive, it may occasionally be worth the $5 monthly charge Ablesoft wants for its updates.

In football, automatic updating is a difficult feature to sell because prices are so volatile. A better option might be to follow your hottest cards via printed price guides. Collectors don't need to scan prices every month to detect trends. Once in a while will do.

Besides, sometimes it's more fun to buy cards, wait a couple years, and see how you did. Even hard-bit-

Many dealers can authenticate rare and highly sought football cards, like this Bart Starr rookie. *Pictured:* 1957 Topps Bart Starr #119.

ten investor/collector types like to tease themselves a little.

One thing that should be noted about these programs is that if you have the free time to put your entire card collection on a computer program, you have a lot of free time.

The sports card buyer's club is a concept that has snagged growing numbers of collectors. Two major clubs operating in the early 1990s were sponsored by *Tuff Stuff* magazine and Yankee Management. Of the two, the $5.95 Yankee Management plan seemed to offer the better deal.

The buyer's club operates on the old principle that a lot of any item can be bought cheaper than a small amount. The buyer's club buys or gets an option to buy cards in large quantity. It then offers these cards to club members at a price lower than what might be expected from a dealer interested in making a profit.

How is a buyer's club different from a regular dealer? Other than the fact that a buyer's club makes you pay a fee up front for the privilege of buying cards, there appears to be little difference between the two. Are the discounts enough to make the initial fee a good investment?

Tuff Stuff's club is truly a bad bargain. Card collectors are asked to shell out a $10 fee for an ID card. The ID card allows the member to get a 10 percent discount at card shops that agree to honor the card.

Card shops honoring the Tuff Stuff Buyer's Club card are few and paltry. A huge state like California, with more than 20 million people, has only 15 shops honoring Tuff Stuff Buyer's Club cards. Save your money.

The Tuff Stuff Buyer's Club appears to be a way for the magazine to goose profits without having to do honest work, and its existence is an unbecoming blemish on an otherwise respected hobby journal.

The last service worth examining is the professional sports card authenticator service. The most well-known of the services is PSA, famed for grading the Gretzky/McNall copy of baseball's T-206 Honus Wagner card.

PSA promises that razor-sharp card experts will check your card to determine if it is altered or counterfeit. They examine your card under a microscope or jeweler's loupe to see how well it matches up with a certified mint edition of the original. They search for subtle differences in print, cardboard shavings signaling an alteration, and similar defects.

Many dealers can also authenti-

If you want a National Chicle card graded, by all means call a service. *Pictured:* 1935 National Chicle Clarke Hinkle #24.

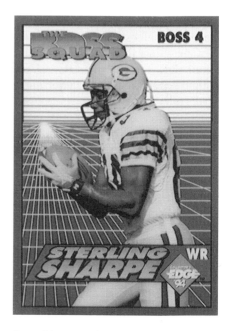

Collectors want cards to remain pristine. *Pictured:* 1994 Playoff Ground Attack Emmitt Smith.

The golden age of football cards has inspired many new products. *Pictured:* 1994 Collectors Edge Sterling Sharpe Boss 4.

cate cards. PSA simply promises to do the very best job of it. If you have a 1935 National Chicle Nagurski you want authenticated, then by all means call PSA. If not, just buy a magnifying glass.

Trading card collecting in general and football card collecting in particular have spawned a wide range of third-party products to help collectors enjoy their hobby. Most of the trading card peripherals now being sold exist because they fill the needs of collectors.

Collectors want their collections to remain pristine. Sad to say, no collection stays perfect forever, but most collectors don't want their collections to decline for lack of effort. Besides being economical, many of the products offered to collectors as adjuncts to card collecting are inventive and well-made, if not downright ingenious. The same imagination animating the new "golden age" of football cards has also inspired new products and services to make collecting more fun than ever.

CHAPTER TWENTY

RESEARCH IT YOURSELF

How to Become an Expert Collector

My "Gridiron Report" column for *Tuff Stuff* ran from 1992 to 1993, under the supervision of editor Tucker Freeman Smith. As a columnist for a national sports card collecting monthly, I often received letters asking questions about players and cards. Invariably the questions required large amounts of time-consuming research. Many of these letters arrived without a self-addressed stamped envelope for reply. It seemed curious to me that people did not wish to undertake these research projects themselves. After all, finding out for yourself is the fun of collecting.

Besides, no one can be a complete repository of the answers to collectors' questions. For that reason, I believe it might be useful to outline some of the methods collectors can use to try to get their own answers.

It turns out that collectors almost always have their own angle, their own slant on collecting. No two card collectors are exactly alike. What people want from the hobby is as unique as a fingerprint.

But often people seem to be puzzled about how to get correct answers to their questions.

In football card collecting there are two things collectors usually want to know: the history of the players and facts about the cards.

Three tools are commonly used to get answers to collecting questions: the library, the telephone call, and the personal letter.

Consider a typical collecting case: Suppose you restrict your football collecting to cards and memorabilia of former West Virginia University football players. This includes cards, coins, stamps, autographs, and even helmets and jerseys.

A trip to the library reveals that a man named Bill Fiske wrote a book on the subject, *West Virginia Sports Memorabilia*. In the book Fiske compiled a very thorough checklist of former Mountaineers who have appeared on sports cards. The book also provides checklists for programs, media guides, and other items. As a collector of WVU materials, you can base your collecting on a book of this sort as the basic text.

After that a phone call to the West Virginia University sports information director might be useful, if only to obtain the exact mailing addresses of additional information sources. For instance, if you wanted to get an autograph from a former college player, the school would be the place to ask. Colleges usually keep extensive lists of alumni addresses and make them available to legitimate queries. Moreover, universities themselves are good places to do re-search, as they are designed for that.

But whenever you need information, you should look first in the books.

Many card hobby books exist. Foremost is Jefferson Burdick's *American Card Catalog*, the seminal text on card collecting and a handy reference for anyone interested in cards. Literally hundreds of other books exist on collecting hobbies. Any library will have scads of them, ranging from detailed histories of Depression glass to extensive volumes on toys, dolls, stamps, coins, and many other collectibles.

There are at least a dozen books covering the subject of baseball cards. A huge supply of magazines also lines the store shelves. Beckett Publications alone offers monthly price guides on no less than four major sports. Krause Publications sells at least six trading card magazines, including the well-known *Sports Cards*.

Hobby books are easily available at local libraries. Some libraries will have subscriptions to the magazines as well.

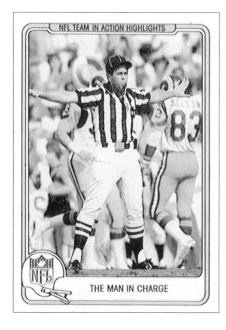

Collectors all have their own slant on collecting football cards. *Pictured: 1982 Fleer Team in Action Jerry Markbright #78 front and reverse.*

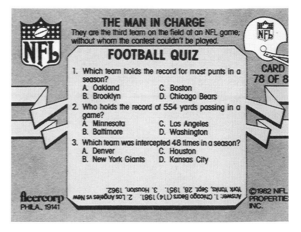

But collectors should be careful about their sources. Price guides are generally useful, but a common drawback of the guides is that they sometimes ignore sets or cards that have major significance.

For example, a glance at Allan Kaye and Michael McKeever's *1994 Football Card Price Guide* published by Avon in their hugely successful Confident Collector series reveals the omission of the 1892 Mayo and 1935 National Chicle sets.

Co-author McKeever admits leaving out the National Chicle set was probably a mistake. "Looking back on it now," McKeever says, "I'm sorry we didn't include the Chicle set."

Nationally distributed issues like the Mayo and National Chicle sets deserve inclusion in any comprehensive handbook.

Reading all there is about football is another good way to increase your hobby knowledge. Making selections from among the vast quantity of football cards is largely guesswork. But collectors can reduce some of the risk by making themselves experts on the sport of football. In plain truth a good way to lose money is to try collecting something you don't know much about. It's like trying to drive without first learning how to operate a car.

Fortunately, many libraries are treasure-troves of basic material on football. Collectors will find player memoirs the best source of straight

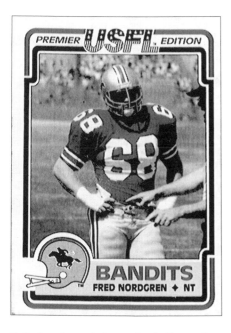

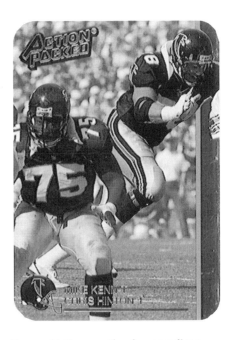

Collectors have to know football to make good decisions about football cards. *Pictured:* 1984 Topps USFL Fred Nordgren #122.

Personal letters are the cheapest direct way to request information. *Pictured:* 1992 Action Packed Mike Kenn/Chris Hinton #10.

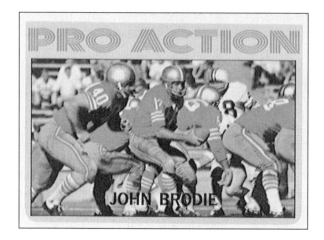

Thoughtful collectors will not make unreasonable demands on former athletes. *Pictured:* 1972 Topps John Brodie #124 front and reverse.

information on the game. It is remarkable how candid these writers are in their opinions of coaches, teammates, and opponents. Also highly recommended are books dealing with the early years of football, as these are the most objective.

You can also find books about football on the racks of used bookstores. NFL annuals like the ones published by *The Sporting News* are excellent sources of accurate and detailed statistical information. Other books, like pictorials and player biographies, generally provide collectors with authentic firsthand stories. Once again, the library heads the list of places football card collectors can go for information.

Personal letters are probably the best and cheapest direct way to find out what you want to know about cards.

Collectors who want a reply must always send a self-addressed, stamped envelope. It is the courteous thing to do. People who handle large volumes of inquiries appreciate SASEs, as they are called. It saves time and effort on the part of the busy correspondent. A letter with an SASE gets answered first, and including an SASE marks the sender as a serious person deserving of attention.

Letters requesting information should be less than one page long. Anything else is overkill. If all you want to write is a fan letter, any length is fine. But for letters asking for specific information, the proper length is less than a page. Try to be concise.

The telephone is an expensive tool, to be used only when you have to get the story straight from the source.

When a collector needs to make a call, either to a sports personality or to a dealer, the secret is to *be prepared.* Know in advance what you are going to ask. If you're in doubt, write it down beforehand. Make sure your notes are handy when you place the call, and learn to leave brief, crisp messages on answering machines and voice mail.

Retired professional players are surprisingly easy to contact by telephone. But don't abuse this knowledge by calling all your favorites and making yourself a pest. Respect the privacy of former players and remember that if they've told the story once, no doubt they've told it a hundred times.

In the 1988 film *Everybody's All-American,* Dennis Quaid plays a former football star who must tell a handful of old football stories to every new acquaintance. By the end of the movie, the Quaid character disappears as a human being. Instead he becomes a machine who tells old football stories over and over simply to please his legion of fans.

In real life, thoughtful football card collectors and fans will not make unreasonable demands on former athletes. Like all of us, they have a right to privacy. They should be treated with the respect due anyone who has achieved success in a difficult field.

Perhaps the most important research project you can undertake is locating an obscure but highly sought card or set that you simply must have for one reason or another. The best and frequently the only way to find it is by phone.

Most hobby magazines will have advertisements for card shops and specialty collectors. To find the cards you want, you should make a list of likely places to call and start calling. Ask the dealer: Do you have any of these cards? Or this particular set? Do you know anyone who does? How much would it cost?

Eventually there will be someone who has seen the cards you seek or knows where they are. Beginning your search at the point of origin, like

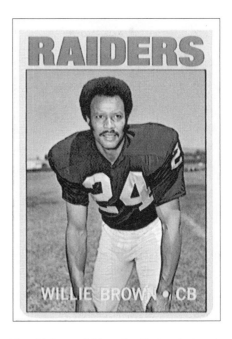

The driving ambition of collectors is to get that card or set that they simply must have. *Pictured:* 1972 Topps Willie Brown #28.

the team's city, seems to help. It requires energy for things to go places. Quite often material things, like people, never seem to leave home. Inertia is your ally.

There are exceptions. No one in Sacramento was able to find the 1991 American Airlines Sacramento Surge minor issue set I sought for nearly two years. Though I combed the capital of the Bear Flag Republic by phone many times, I failed to turn one up. It wasn't until I stretched the net to include Los Angeles that I was successful.

In the end, collectors can save themselves time and money by developing the rudimentary skills of journalism. Just about every question has an answer somewhere. Finding out where the answers are is the best way hobbyists can make the system of collectors, dealers, price guides, and product truly work for them.

CHAPTER TWENTY-ONE

REFLECTIONS ON FOOTBALL CARD COLLECTING

Major League Sport and Popular Culture Converge

Football cards started as a premium companies used to sell tobacco and have developed into a modern imaging industry showcasing the latest and most spectacular graphics innovations. No wonder the hobby has drawn millions of new enthusiasts, many of them attracted by the high quality of recent cards. It is as if the hobby has entered a more confident, secure era. We can be cynical about the massive numbers of cards coming out, but by their purchases collectors have said that they like the new cards and like them a lot.

Football cards have indeed come a long way from the crude specimens first issued over a century ago. Modern cards bear only a faint resemblance to football cards issued as recently as the late 1940s. Sophisticated graphic techniques using computers have revolutionized printing in general and trading cards in particular.

If truth be told, there really weren't many good football cards made before 1989. The Mayo Cut Plug cards have a strong historical interest but differ little from other tobacco-era cards.

The National Chicle cards are an exceptionally fine series, in spite of their small size. These full-color cards were made from oil paintings based on photographs made of the players, and the results are excellent. The National Chicle cards have a

Modern cards showcase the latest graphics. *Pictured:* 1994 Topps Finest Roger Craig #181.

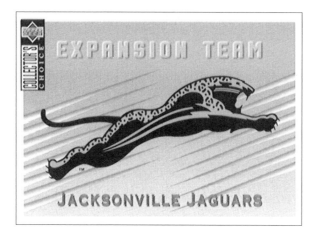

Modern cards bear only a faint resemblance to cards made as recently as the 1940s. *Pictured:* 1994 Upper Deck Jacksonville Jaguars #380.

quality about them second to none. That's why they will always hold up as coveted collectibles in our hobby.

In the early 1950s, Bowman put together a batch of superb sets. The 1950, 1951, and 1952 sets are pillars of the hobby. It is possible that modern collectors may someday "redis-

Football cards have come a long way from the specimens issued a century ago. *Pictured, from left to right:* 1892 Mayo Cut Plug Wrightington and 1992 Collectors Edge Jim Kelly #7.

The National Chicle cards are a fine series. *Pictured:* **1935 National Chicle Bo Molenda #2.**

Finally, the entry of Topps into the premium card market through its Stadium Club series has been well-received by football card collectors. The Stadium Club cards are fast becoming the definitive premium card, in spite of efforts by competitors like Fleer to one-up the Stadium Club style.

The hobby appears to have made a strong favorable decision about the 1989 Score and 1992 Bowman sets as well. Although the quality of the 1989 Score cards was quickly surpassed by others, Score forever made a niche for itself in the hobby by issuing this fine 330-card set at a key moment in hobby history.

Collecting football cards is a hobby once considered to be child-

cover" the early Bowman product, thus pushing prices for these cards right into the stratosphere.

Although in the main Topps Chewing Gum has produced mediocre cards at best, the company that held a 20-year monopoly hasn't been entirely derelict in producing significant football sets.

Topps gets credit for making one of the best card sets in history, the brilliant Topps 1965 AFL set. Another superior Topps product is the 263-card 1971 NFL set, known for a clean and effective design and containing the first card of Steeler great Terry Bradshaw.

Topps also deserves kudos for the 1984 and 1985 USFL sets, which are outstanding both as history and as card art. The 1984 Topps USFL set especially will probably always be highly sought because of its well-executed design and player selection.

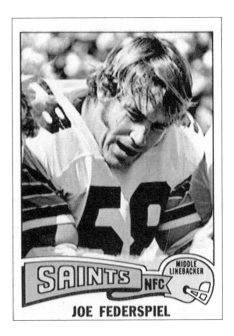

Topps gets credit for making football cards when nobody else was doing it. *Pictured:* **1975 Joe Federspiel #107.**

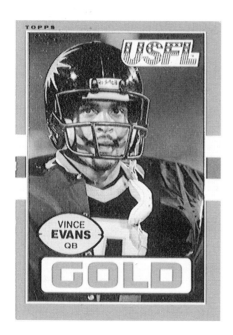

The hobby has made a strong favorable decision on the Topps USFL sets and the 1992 Bowman cards. *Pictured, from left to right:* 1985 Topps USFL Vince Evans #31 and 1992 Bowman Jeff Bostic #345.

ish. It isn't any more. Hobbies answer a deep need in people to be connected to something larger than themselves, in however small a way.

Collecting football cards is a serious hobby, but how do football cards rate as an investment? In the final analysis, card collecting is not really a way to make money. A card or a set you own may soar in value. The card you bought for a dime yesterday may suddenly rise to a value of several hundred dollars or more.

It happens.

But sports cards will never be the equivalent of blue chip stocks, mutual funds, or money market certificates. Collectors of football cards and similar items may attach value to them, but we know they have no intrinsic value. Cards cannot be eaten, worn, or used for transportation. They are too small to make good decorations for the walls of your hut. A couple hundred years from now, they will probably not even exist, save in a vault in some forgotten museum.

Paper securities like stocks at least represent something real. They are a piece of a company or business that makes goods or provides services for a profit. Sports cards exist for the purpose of hero worship alone. It's like keeping a picture of your boyfriend or girlfriend as a personal memento. Valued, but not valuable.

Card prices, on the other hand, chiefly exist to determine who's hot and who's not. If all the cards had zero value, as they did in the old

162

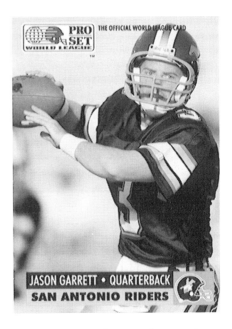

Hobbies answer a human need to be connected to something larger than oneself. *Pictured:* 1992 Score Pinnacle Craig Heyward #192.

The card you bought yesterday may rise to a value of several hundred dollars. It happens. *Pictured:* 1991 Pro Set World League Jason Garrett #143.

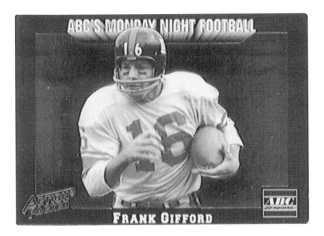

Sports cards' ultimate purpose is hero worship alone. *Pictured:* 1993 Action Packed Monday Night Football Frank Gifford #80.

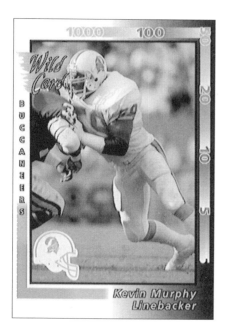

Some 17 billion sports cards were printed in 1992. That's a pretty fair market in memories. *Pictured:* 1992 Wild Card Kevin Murphy #48.

chiefly with commons and having only a few stars. Our hobby has no equivalent of Ty Cobb, Honus Wagner, or Babe Ruth. The closest we come is Bronko Nagurski, Knute Rockne, and Joe Namath.

To illustrate, take a quick peek at the numbers: From the release of the first football card in 1888 to the year 1988, just about 15,000 mainstream football cards were produced, including the Mayo Cut Plug and National Chicle sets. A smaller number of minor issues supplemented the cards made by the big guys, for a total of around 25,000 different football cards. Today fewer than 200 of these cards cost over $50.

This tells us that football card collectors are collecting more for fun

days, they would still be collected. People like cards to remind them of those who played the game. In 1992 some 17 billion sports cards were printed in North America. That's a pretty fair market in memories.

Right now the emphasis is on newer football cards because they are so much better technically than the old cards. The old cards might be better as investments, but modern collectors haven't yet agreed. Their hobby dollars say that we are now in the golden age of sports and sports card collecting.

In some significant respects, the football card hobby differs from the hobby practiced by our cousins in baseball. We are a predominantly blue-collar enterprise, concerned

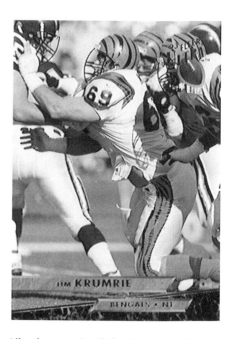

Like the sport itself, football card collecting is a blue-collar enterprise, with many commons—like this 1993 Fleer Ultra Tim Krumrie #60—and few stars.

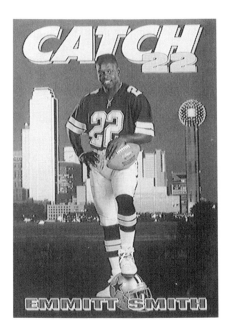

Collectors are doing it more for fun than profit. *Pictured:* 1992 SkyBox PrimeTime Emmitt Smith #165.

than profit. We collect cards because of the pleasure it brings us, not as an investment. Owning a nice set of football cards helps us arrange the game in our minds and lets us participate more fully as spectators.

There's not much more you can ask of a hobby.

PRICE GUIDES

100 KEY
FOOTBALL CARDS

In the following pages, I have listed what I consider to be the 100 key football cards made for the hobby in North America since 1888. This list includes rare pre–World War II cards, some fairly obscure cards from minor issue sets, and Canadian cards. For the sake of simplicity, I have eliminated all coins, stamps, labels, and other such novelty items.

I also left out the second-year cards of many star players, instead focusing on the first-issue cards of those players. I wanted to isolate the key football cards in the hobby, not just the most expensive. In many cases the high-value cards are key cards, though not always.

For example, Jim Brown's key card is his rookie card, #62 in the Topps 1958 NFL set. The price on this card is $500. His second-year card, #10 in the 1959 Topps set, is also quite valuable at about $175. But in this list, I've left out the second-year card for because other Brown cards are more significant.

Let me add the standard disclaimer: Any list of this sort is a strictly subjective exercise, prepared only for the edification of the reader. Also, these prices reflect the maximum a collector would expect to pay for a top-grade specimen and, as such, may vary from those in the general price guide.

Rank	Year	Maker	Number	Name	Price
1	1935	National Chicle	#34	Bronko Nagurski	$9,000
2	1935	National Chicle	#9	Knute Rockne	$3,000
3	1952	Bowman Large	#144	Jim Lansford	$2,800
4	1965	Topps AFL	#122	Joe Namath	$1,500
5	1935	National Chicle	#36	Bernie Masterson	$1,250
6	1933	Goudey	#4	Red Grange	$900
7	1933	Goudey	#6	Jim Thorpe	$800
8	1935	National Chicle	#1	Dutch Clark	$700
9	1952	Bowman Large	#16	Frank Gifford	$600
10	1957	Topps	#138	John Unitas	$600

Rank	Year	Maker	Number	Name	Price
11	1951	Bowman	#20	Tom Landry	$500
12	1957	Topps	#119	Bart Starr	$500
13	1892	Mayo Cut Plug	#35	John Dunlop	$500
14	1888	Old Judge		Henry Beecher	$500
15	1958	Topps	#62	Jim Brown	$500
16	1957	Topps	#151	Paul Hornung	$500
17	1983	Jogo CFL	#91	Warren Moon	$400
18	1961	National City	#2	Jim Brown	$400
19	1962	Topps	#90	Fran Tarkenton	$400
20	1948	Bowman	#108	Buford Ray	$400
21	1966	Philadelphia	#38	Gale Sayers	$350
22	1950	Topps Feltback	#64	Joe Paterno	$350
23	1948	Bowman	#22	Sammy Baugh	$350
24	1962	Post Cereal	#74	Sam Baker	$350
25	1935	National Chicle	#26	John Dell Isola	$350
26	1935	National Chicle	#27	Bull Tosi	$350
27	1935	National Chicle	#28	Stan Kosta	$350
28	1948	Leaf	#34	Sammy Baugh	$350
29	1935	National Chicle	#30	Ernie Caddel	$350
30	1935	National Chicle	#31	Nic Niccola	$350
31	1935	National Chicle	#32	Swede Johnston	$350
32	1935	National Chicle	#29	Jim MacMurdo	$350
33	1935	National Chicle	#33	Ernie Smith	$350
34	1954	Bowman	#23	George Blanda	$300
35	1950	Bowman	#5	Y. A. Tittle	$300
36	1948	Leaf	#73	Jackie Jensen	$300
37	1955	Topps All-American	#37	Jim Thorpe	$300
38	1955	Topps All-American	#68	Four Horsemen	$300
39	1960	Fleer	#124	Jack Kemp	$300
40	1935	National Chicle	#25	Dale Burnett	$300
41	1967	Royal Castle	#10	Bob Griese	$250
42	1948	Leaf	#1	Sid Luckman	$200
43	1984	Topps USFL	#36	Jim Kelly	$200
44	1976	Topps	#148	Walter Payton	$200
45	1954	Blue Ribbon Tea CFL	#7	Bud Grant	$200
46	1948	Leaf	#26	Bob Waterfield	$200
47	1970	Topps	#90	O. J. Simpson	$200
48	1951	Bowman	#4	Norm Van Brocklin	$200
49	1952	Bowman Large	#127	Ollie Matson	$200
50	1948	Bowman	#3	John Lujack	$200
51	1948	Bowman	#12	Charlie Conerly	$200
52	1948	Leaf	#6	Bobby Layne	$200
53	1948	Bowman	#63	Pete Pihos	$200

Rank	Year	Maker	Number	Name	Price
54	1981	Topps	#216	Joe Montana	$200
55	1948	Bowman	#8	Kenny Washington	$150
56	1959	Wheaties CFL	#15	Russ Jackson	$150
57	1948	Bowman	#26	Bob Waterfield	$150
58	1948	Leaf	#52	Leo Nomellini	$150
59	1948	Leaf	#53	Charlie Conerly	$150
60	1948	Leaf	#54	Chuck Bednarik	$150
61	1935	National Chicle	#24	Clarke Hinkle	$150
62	1935	National Chicle	#22	Shipwreck Kelley	$150
63	1935	National Chicle	#10	Cliff Battles	$150
64	1960	Kahn's	#2	Jim Brown	$150
65	1966	Philadelphia	#31	Dick Butkus	$150
66	1988	Pro Set Test	#2	Jerry Rice	$150
67	1962	Post Cereal	#193	Joe Krakoski	$150
68	1952	Bowman Large	#14	Paul Brown	$150
69	1956	Shredded Wheat CFL	#87	Normie Kwong	$150
70	1961	Topps	#150	Don Maynard	$150
71	1972	Topps	#200	Roger Staubach	$150
72	1948	Bowman	#107	Sid Luckman	$150
73	1950	Bowman	#45	Otto Graham	$150
74	1952	Bowman Large	#29	Hugh McElhenny	$150
75	1952	Bowman Large	#46	Art Donovan	$150
76	1950	Bowman	#35	Joe Perry	$150
77	1950	Bowman	#43	Marion Motley	$150
78	1948	Bowman	#1	Joe Tereshinski	$150
79	1948	Bowman	#99	Harry Gilmer	$150
80	1961	Fleer	#41	Don Meredith	$150
81	1963	Fleer	#47	Len Dawson	$150
82	1984	Topps	#123	Dan Marino	$100
83	1981	Topps	#194	Art Monk	$100
84	1984	Topps USFL	#52	Steve Young	$100
85	1986	Topps	#161	Jerry Rice	$100
86	1971	OPC	#13	Joe Theismann	$100
87	1948	Bowman	#36	Bulldog Turner	$100
88	1935	National Chicle	#23	Beattie Feathers	$100
89	1948	Leaf	#19A	George McAfee	$100
90	1969	Topps	#26	Brian Piccolo	$100
91	1959	Wheaties CFL	#33	Hal Patterson	$100
92	1952	Bowman Large	#48	George Halas	$100
93	1984	Topps USFL	#74	Herschel Walker	$50
94	1984	Topps USFL	#58	Reggie White	$50
95	1977	Topps	#177	Steve Largent	$50
96	1952	Parkhurst CFL	#42	Sam Etcheverry	$50

Rank	Year	Maker	Number	Name	Price
97	1975	Topps	#367	Dan Fouts	$50
98	1959	Topps	#103	Alex Karras	$50
99	1963	Topps	#82	Bob Lilly	$50
100	1963	Fleer	#72	Lance Alworth	$50

FOOTBALL CARD PRICE GUIDE

1892–1994

In the following pages, prices are listed for every mainstream football card set of the first 100 years of football card collecting. By coincidence, there are about as many major sets as there are years. Each listing is made up of the following elements: the year the set was issued; the maker of the set; the total number of cards in the set (listed in parentheses after "Complete Set"); the current market price for a complete set; the current market price for a common card; and the current market prices for several individual cards, listed by number and name. In some cases, a specialty set is listed under a given manufacturer, along with the number of cards in that set and some of the individual cards included in it. (The number of cards in the specialty set is not included in the total for the com-

plete set.) A special (*R*) designation next to an individual card indicates that the card is generally considered to be the player's first card, also known as the rookie card.

Prices are listed for two grades of condition—very good and near-mint. Not many collectors desire cards in lesser grades, often accepting them only when cost or availability make such aquisitions otherwise impossible.

A near-mint card has only one tiny flaw, usually a fuzzy corner or a slight off-centering. Most older cards that are in top grades are near-mint cards.

A very good card is one that shows evidence of human handling but usually no major wear. Very good cards are valued at about 25 percent of mint to near-mint.

CURRENT PRICES FOR CARDS
IN VERY GOOD OR NEAR-MINT CONDITION

Cards (listed by year and maker)	Very Good	Near Mint
1890s Mayo Cut Plug Tobacco		
Complete Set (35)	$3,500.00	$14,000.00
Common Player	200.00	500.00
George Adee (*R*)	150.00	600.00

Cards (listed by year and maker)	Very Good	Near Mint

1890s Mayo Cut Plug Tobacco (*Continued*)

	Very Good	Near Mint
Edgar Poe *(R)*	150.00	600.00
Frank Hinkey *(R)*	200.00	700.00
John Dunlop *(R)*	250.00	800.00
Doggie Trenchard *(R)*	275.00	700.00

1935 National Chicle Gum

	Very Good	Near Mint
Complete Set (36)	4,000.00	16,000.00
Common Player	50.00	200.00
#1 Earl Dutch Clark *(R)*	75.00	300.00
#9 Knute Rockne *(R)*	700.00	3,000.00
#34 Bronko Nagurski *(R)*	2,500.00	9,000.00
#36 Bernie Masterson *(R)*	400.00	1,300.00

1948 Bowman

	Very Good	Near Mint
Complete Set (108)	2,000.00	7,500.00
Common Player	16.00	50.00
#3 Johnny Lujack *(R)*	80.00	300.00
#8 Kenny Washington *(R)*	50.00	200.00
#12 Charlie Conerly *(R)*	75.00	300.00
#22 Sammy Baugh *(R)*	100.00	350.00
#108 Buford Ray *(R)*	150.00	500.00

1948 Leaf

	Very Good	Near Mint
Complete Set (98)	3,750.00	7,000.00
Common Player	2.50	10.00
#1 Sid Luckman *(R)*	75.00	250.00
#6 Bobby Layne *(R)*	100.00	400.00
#17A Kenny Washington *(R)*	50.00	200.00
#17B Kenny Washington *(R)*	50.00	200.00
#34 Sammy Baugh *(R)*	110.00	350.00
#52 Leo Nomellini *(R)*	50.00	200.00
#53 Charlie Conerly *(R)*	50.00	200.00
#54 Chuck Bednarik *(R)*	50.00	200.00
#73 Jackie Jensen *(R)*	55.00	220.00

1949 Leaf

	Very Good	Near Mint
Complete Set (49)	350.00	1,600.00
Common Player	2.00	10.00
#15 Sid Luckman	40.00	140.00
#26 Sammy Baugh	45.00	150.00
#67 Bobby Layne	35.00	175.00
#134 Chuck Bednarik	17.00	65.00

Cards (listed by year and maker)	Very Good	Near Mint
1949 Leaf (*Continued*)		
#150 Bulldog Turner	25.00	100.00
1950 Bowman		
Complete Set (144)	900.00	3,600.00
Common Player	2.50	10.00
#5 Y. A. Tittle *(R)*	60.00	250.00
#6 Lou Groza *(R)*	32.50	130.00
#16 Glenn Davis *(R)*	25.00	100.00
#35 Joe Perry *(R)*	25.00	100.00
#37 Bobby Layne	38.00	150.00
#43 Marion Motley *(R)*	25.00	100.00
#45 Otto Graham *(R)*	100.00	400.00
#52 Elroy Hirsch	25.00	100.00
#100 Sammy Baugh	31.00	125.00
1951 Bowman		
Complete Set (144)	750.00	3,000.00
Common Player	2.50	10.00
#2 Otto Graham	25.00	100.00
#4 Norm Van Brocklin *(R)*	38.00	150.00
#20 Tom Landry *(R)*	120.00	500.00
#34 Sammy Baugh	30.00	125.00
#91 Emlen Tunnell *(R)*	18.00	72.00
#102 Bobby Layne	25.00	100.00
#109 Marion Motley	25.00	100.00
1952 Bowman Large		
Complete Set (144)	3,000.00	12,000.00
Common Player	4.00	15.00
#1 Norm Van Brocklin	75.00	300.00
#2 Otto Graham	50.00	200.00
#16 Frank Gifford *(R)*	175.00	700.00
#17 Y. A. Tittle	38.00	150.00
#27 Bob Miller *(R)*	63.00	250.00
#28 Kyle Rote *(R)*	38.00	150.00
#29 Hugh McElhenny *(R)*	25.00	100.00
#30 Sammy Baugh	63.00	250.00
#36 John Lee Hancock *(R)*	75.00	300.00
#45 Steve Van Buren	38.00	150.00
#46 Art Donovan *(R)*	25.00	100.00
#48 George Halas *(R)*	25.00	100.00
#78 Bobby Layne	63.00	150.00

Cards (listed by year and maker)	Very Good	Near Mint
1952 Bowman Large (*Continued*)		
#99 Joe Stydahar *(R)*	120.00	500.00
#108 Hubert Johnston *(R)*	80.00	350.00
#127 Ollie Matson	50.00	200.00
#135 Gene Ronzani *(R)*	100.00	400.00
#142 Tom Landry	120.00	500.00
#144 Jim Lansford *(R)*	900.00	3,500.00
1952 Bowman Small		
Complete Set (144)	1,150.00	4,500.00
Common Player	2.50	10.00
#1 Norm Van Brocklin	50.00	200.00
#2 Otto Graham	30.00	125.00
#16 Frank Gifford *(R)*	120.00	500.00
#30 Sammy Baugh	35.00	140.00
#48 George Halas *(R)*	17.00	70.00
#142 Tom Landry	25.00	100.00
#144 Jim Lansford *(R)*	35.00	140.00
1953 Bowman		
Complete Set (96)	600.00	2,400.00
Common Player	2.50	10.00
#1 Eddie LeBaron *(R)*	40.00	160.00
#11 Norm Van Brocklin	20.00	100.00
#26 Otto Graham	35.00	120.00
#43 Frank Gifford	75.00	300.00
#95 Lou Groza	25.00	100.00
1954 Bowman		
Complete Set (128)	400.00	1,600.00
Common Player	1.50	5.00
#11 Zeke Bratkowski *(R)*	7.00	29.00
#23 George Blanda *(R)*	75.00	300.00
#55 Frank Gifford	25.00	100.00
#128 John Lattner *(R)*	25.00	100.00
1955 Bowman		
Complete Set (160)	400.00	1,500.00
Common Player	1.00	3.00
#7 Frank Gifford	25.00	100.00
#8 Alan Ameche *(R)*	7.00	26.00
#62 George Blanda	25.00	100.00
#152 Tom Landry	35.00	130.00

Cards (listed by year and maker)	Very Good	Near Mint
1956 Topps		
Complete Set (120)	450.00	1,700.00
Common Player	1.25	4.00
#5 Alex Webster (R)	1.30	5.00
#6 Norm Van Brocklin	6.00	25.00
#11 George Blanda	25.00	100.00
#44 Joe Schmidt (R)	15.00	45.00
#53 Frank Gifford	40.00	150.00
#101 Rosey Grier	8.00	30.00
XX Checklist	100.00	400.00
1957 Topps		
Complete Set (154)	700.00	2,800.00
Common Player	1.00	2.50
#1 Eddie LeBaron	20.00	75.00
#30 Y. A. Tittle	16.00	60.00
#88 Frank Gifford	25.00	100.00
#119 Bart Starr (R)	125.00	500.00
#138 John Unitas (R)	120.00	500.00
#151 Paul Hornung (R)	120.00	500.00
XX Checklist	170.00	700.00
1958 Topps		
Complete Set (132)	330.00	1,200.00
Common Player	.80	2.00
#22 John Unitas	50.00	200.00
#62 Jim Brown (R)	150.00	700.00
#66 Bart Starr	65.00	140.00
#73 Frank Gifford	25.00	100.00
#86 Y. A. Tittle	8.00	33.00
#90 Sonny Jurgensen (R)	30.00	125.00
1959 Topps		
Complete Set (176)	275.00	1,100.00
Common Player	.50	1.20
#1 John Unitas	25.00	100.00
#10 Jim Brown	50.00	200.00
#51 Sam Huff (R)	15.00	60.00
#82 Paul Hornung	15.00	60.00
#103 Alex Karras (R)	20.00	75.00
#105 John David Crow (R)	1.50	5.00

Cards (listed by year and maker)	Very Good	Near Mint
1960 Fleer AFL		
Complete Set (132)	150.00	700.00
Common Player	.50	1.00
#58 George Blanda	8.00	35.00
#118 Ron Mix *(R)*	8.20	36.00
#124 Jack Kemp *(R)*	100.00	350.00
1960 Topps NFL		
Complete Set (132)	150.00	700.00
Common Player	.50	1.00
#1 John Unitas	25.00	100.00
#23 Jim Brown	25.00	100.00
#51 Bart Starr	8.00	30.00
#52 Jim Taylor	2.50	10.00
#56 Forrest Gregg *(R)*	8.00	32.00
1961 Fleer AFL-NFL		
Complete Set (220)	350.00	1,400.00
Common Player	1.00	2.00
#11 Jim Brown	25.00	100.00
#31 Alan Ameche	2.00	9.00
#40 Eddie LeBaron	.75	3.00
#41 Don Meredith *(R)*	38.00	150.00
#59 John Brodie *(R)*	12.00	50.00
#88 Bart Starr	8.00	29.00
#155 Jack Kemp	50.00	150.00
#188 Tom Flores *(R)*	4.00	18.00
#215 Don Maynard *(R)*	50.00	200.00
1961 Topps AFL-NFL		
Complete Set (197)	250.00	1,100.00
Common Player	1.00	2.00
#1 John Unitas	20.00	80.00
#35 Alex Karras	8.00	35.00
#40 Paul Hornung	7.00	30.00
#58 Y. A. Tittle	6.00	25.00
#67 Checklist	8.00	30.00
#71 Jim Brown	20.00	75.00
#166 Jack Kemp	25.00	100.00
#198 Checklist	18.00	75.00
1962 Fleer AFL		
Complete Set (88)	200.00	700.00
Common Player	.50	1.00

Cards (listed by year and maker)	Very Good	Near Mint
1962 Fleer AFL (*Continued*)		
#3 Gino Capelletti *(R)*	3.00	13.00
#46 George Blanda	12.00	40.00
#79 Jack Kemp	25.00	100.00
#82 Ron Mix	2.00	8.00
#86 Ernie Ladd *(R)*	4.00	15.00
1962 Topps NFL		
Complete Set (176)	400.00	1,600.00
Common Player	1.00	2.00
#1 Johnny Unitas	25.00	100.00
#17 Mike Ditka	25.00	100.00
#28 Jim Brown	30.00	120.00
#39 Don Meredith	20.00	80.00
#88 Roman Gabriel *(R)*	7.00	29.00
#90 Fran Tarkenton *(R)*	120.00	450.00
#104 Frank Gifford	12.00	45.00
#151 Billy Kilmer *(R)*	5.00	18.00
#176 Checklist	25.00	100.00
1963 Fleer AFL		
Complete Set (88)	400.00	1,600.00
Common Player	1.00	2.00
#2 Babe Parilli	2.00	8.00
#6 Charles Long *(R)*	50.00	200.00
#10 Nick Buoniconti *(R)*	10.00	45.00
#23 Cookie Gilchrist *(R)*	4.00	17.00
#24 Jack Kemp	30.00	120.00
#47 Len Dawson *(R)*	40.00	160.00
#48 Abner Hayes	2.00	8.50
#64 Bob Dougherty *(R)*	55.00	220.00
#72 Lance Alworth *(R)*	37.00	155.00
XX Checklist	100.00	400.00
1963 Topps NFL		
Complete Set (170)	275.00	1,100.00
Common Player	.55	1.10
#1 John Unitas	25.00	100.00
#14 Jim Brown	25.00	100.00
#19 Lou Groza	4.00	15.00
#44 Deacon Jones *(R)*	12.00	50.00
#62 Mike Ditka	8.00	35.00
#74 Don Meredith	13.00	40.00

Cards (listed by year and maker)	Very Good	Near Mint
1963 Topps NFL (*Continued*)		
#82 Bob Lilly *(R)*	20.00	80.00
#96 Ray Nitschke	18.00	70.00
#98 Fran Tarkenton	25.00	100.00
#107 Jim Marshall *(R)*	5.00	20.00
#155 Larry Wilson *(R)*	8.50	30.00
#170 Checklist	14.00	50.00
1964 Philadelphia Gum NFL		
Complete Set (198)	250.00	900.00
Common Player	.45	.90
#1 Ray Berry	6.00	25.00
#3 John Mackey *(R)*	4.00	18.00
#12 John Unitas	14.00	50.00
#28 George Halas	3.00	11.00
#30 Jim Brown	18.00	70.00
#51 Don Meredith	10.00	40.00
#71 Herb Adderly *(R)*	15.00	60.00
#80 John Taylor	3.00	12.00
#89 Roman Gabriel	1.25	5.00
#91 Merlin Olsen	18.00	70.00
#109 Fran Tarkenton	14.00	50.00
#117 Frank Gifford	10.00	40.00
1964 Topps AFL		
Complete Set (176)	325.00	1,300.00
Common Player	.75	1.50
#1 Tommy Addison	9.00	36.00
#30 Jack Kemp	27.00	110.00
#31 Daryle Lamonica *(R)*	10.00	40.00
#68 George Blanda	8.50	35.00
#92 Buck Buchanan *(R)*	5.00	20.00
#96 Len Dawson	14.00	55.00
#121 Don Maynard	5.00	20.00
#125 Matt Snell *(R)*	2.50	10.00
#155 Lance Alworth	5.00	20.00
#159 John Hadl *(R)*	2.50	10.00
#176 Checklist	22.00	85.00
1965 Philadelphia Gum NFL		
Complete Set (198)	150.00	700.00
Common Player	.40	.75
#12 John Unitas	13.00	35.00

Cards (listed by year and maker)	Very Good	Near Mint
1965 Philadelphia Gum NFL (*Continued*)		
#31 Jim Brown	15.00	60.00
#41 Paul Warfield *(R)*	12.00	50.00
#53 Mel Renfro *(R)*	3.00	12.00
#84 Vince Lombardi	2.50	10.00
#105 Carl Eller *(R)*	2.50	10.00
#110 Fran Tarkenton	9.00	35.00
#188 Sonny Jurgensen	5.00	20.00
#195 Charley Taylor *(R)*	11.00	45.00
1965 Topps AFL		
Complete Set (176)	880.00	3,500.00
Common Player	2.00	5.00
#1 Tommy Addison	10.00	40.00
#35 Jack Kemp	50.00	200.00
#36 Daryle Lamonica	6.50	22.00
#37 Paul McGuire	5.00	17.00
#46 Willie Brown *(R)*	18.00	70.00
#69 George Blanda	25.00	100.00
#87 Checklist	22.00	90.00
#117 John Huarte *(R)*	5.00	20.00
#122 Joe Namath *(R)*	400.00	1,300.00
#133 Fred Biletnikoff *(R)*	50.00	200.00
#137 Ben Davidson *(R)*	7.50	30.00
#139 Tom Flores	2.50	10.00
#155 Lance Alworth	12.00	45.00
#164 Ernie Ladd	5.00	17.00
#176 Checklist #2	55.00	220.00
1966 Philadelphia Gum NFL		
Complete Set (198)	225.00	900.00
Common Player	.20	.60
#24 John Unitas	8.00	30.00
#31 Dick Butkus *(R)*	40.00	160.00
#38 Gale Sayers *(R)*	63.00	250.00
#41 Jim Brown	13.00	50.00
#61 Don Meredith	10.00	40.00
#88 Bart Starr	8.00	30.00
#114 Fran Tarkenton	8.00	30.00
#198 Checklist #2	6.00	25.00
1966 Topps AFL		
Complete Set (132)	325.00	1,300.00
Common Player	.70	2.00

Cards (listed by year and maker)	Very Good	Near Mint
1966 Topps AFL (*Continued*)		
#15 Funny Ring List	77.00	300.00
#26 Jack Kemp	30.00	100.00
#96 Joe Namath	80.00	300.00
#101 George Sauer Jr.	2.50	10.00
#132 Checklist	19.00	75.00
1967 Philadelphia Gum NFL		
Complete Set (198)	160.00	600.00
Common Player	.30	.75
#7 Tommy Nobis *(R)*	2.00	7.00
#23 John Unitas	7.00	24.00
#28 Dick Butkus	10.00	40.00
#35 Gale Sayers	20.00	75.00
#54 Lee Roy Jordan *(R)*	2.50	10.00
#57 Don Meredith	4.00	18.00
#82 Bart Starr	5.00	20.00
#106 Fran Tarkenton	7.00	24.00
#123 Paul Hornung	4.00	18.00
#185 Sonny Jurgensen	3.00	10.00
#198 Checklist #2	5.00	20.00
1967 Topps AFL		
Complete Set (132)	125.00	500.00
Common Player	.45	1.00
#24 Jack Kemp	7.00	25.00
#59 Checklist	4.00	17.00
#97 Don Maynard	2.50	10.00
#98 Joe Namath	30.00	120.00
#106 Fred Biletnikoff	5.00	20.00
#123 Lance Alworth	3.50	15.00
#132 Checklist	10.00	40.00
1968 Topps AFL-NFL		
Complete Set (219)	150.00	600.00
Common Player	.30	.75
#1 Bart Starr	9.00	35.00
#25 Don Meredith	7.00	25.00
#65 Joe Namath	15.00	60.00
#75 Gale Sayers	25.00	100.00
#100 John Unitas	7.00	25.00
#127 Dick Butkus	8.00	30.00
#142 George Blanda	6.00	20.00

Cards (listed by year and maker)	Very Good	Near Mint

1968 Topps AFL-NFL (Continued)

		Very Good	Near Mint
#149	Jack Kemp	8.00	30.00
#155	Craig Morton (R)	3.00	10.00
#159	Joe Kapp (R)	1.50	5.00
#161	Fran Tarkenton	7.00	25.00
#196	Bob Griese (R)	25.00	100.00

1969 Topps

		Very Good	Near Mint
Complete Set (263)		125.00	500.00
Common Player		.25	.50
#25	John Unitas	7.00	25.00
#26	Brian Piccolo (R)	25.00	100.00
#36	Danny Abramowitz (R)	2.00	5.00
#51	Gale Sayers	15.00	60.00
#75	Don Meredith	6.00	20.00
#80	Checklist	5.50	22.00
#100	Joe Namath	20.00	80.00
#120	Larry Csonka (R)	20.00	70.00
#139	Dick Butkus	5.00	18.00
#150	Fran Tarkenton	6.00	20.00
#161	Bob Griese	3.00	15.00
#215	Bart Starr	4.00	18.00
#232	George Blanda	5.00	20.00

1970 Topps

		Very Good	Near Mint
Complete Set (263)		110.00	425.00
Common Player		.15	.30
#1	Len Dawson	4.00	15.00
#10	Bob Griese	2.50	9.00
#25	Jan Stenerud (R)	1.75	6.00
#30	Bart Starr	7.00	25.00
#59	Alan Page (R)	10.00	38.00
#75	Lem Barney (R)	3.00	10.00
#90	O. J. Simpson (R)	40.00	160.00
#114	Bubba Smith (R)	4.00	15.00
#150	Joe Namath	8.00	45.00
#247	Fred Dryer (R)	4.00	15.00

1971 Topps

		Very Good	Near Mint
Complete Set (263)		110.00	500.00
Common Player		.15	.35
#1	John Unitas	8.00	30.00
#3	Marty Schottenheimer (R)	1.50	5.00

Cards (listed by year and maker)	Very Good	Near Mint
1971 Topps (*Continued*)		
#114 Willie Lanier *(R)*	4.00	15.00
#156 Terry Bradshaw *(R)*	35.00	125.00
#200 Bart Starr	6.00	20.00
#245 Joe Greene *(R)*	8.00	30.00
#250 Joe Namath	10.00	40.00
#260 O. J. Simpson	15.00	45.00
1972 Topps		
Complete Set (351)	480.00	1,900.00
Common Player 1–263	.15	.35
Common Player 263–351	3.00	12.00
#13 John Riggins *(R)*	7.00	25.00
#15 John Hadl	.80	2.00
#18 Billy Kilmer	.80	2.00
#65 Jim Plunkett *(R)*	4.00	15.00
#93 Ted Hendricks *(R)*	4.00	15.00
#100 Joe Namath	25.00	90.00
#106 Lyle Alzado *(R)*	6.00	18.00
#101 L. C. Greenwood *(R)*	4.00	14.00
#110 Gale Sayers	8.00	25.00
#186 Gene Upshaw *(R)*	4.00	15.00
#195 Sonny Jurgensen	1.00	4.00
#200 Roger Staubach *(R)*	28.00	120.00
#244 Charlie Joiner *(R)*	4.50	16.00
#291 Steve Spurrier	5.00	20.00
#343 Joe Namath	65.00	250.00
1973 Topps		
Complete Set (528)	100.00	400.00
Common Player	.15	.30
#34 Ken Anderson *(R)*	10.00	40.00
#77 Art Shell *(R)*	8.00	30.00
#89 Franco Harris *(R)*	15.00	60.00
#115 Jack Ham *(R)*	4.00	15.00
#236 Charley Taylor	1.25	4.00
#322 Dan Dierdorf *(R)*	3.30	12.00
#343 Jack Youngblood *(R)*	3.00	10.00
#400 Joe Namath	8.00	25.00
#475 Roger Staubach	7.50	25.00
#487 Ken Stabler *(R)*	6.00	18.00
#500 O. J. Simpson	6.20	20.00

Cards (listed by year and maker)	**Very Good**	**Near Mint**
1974 Topps		
Complete Set (528)	75.00	275.00
Common Player	.15	.30
#1 O. J. Simpson	5.00	18.00
#105 Ahmad Rashad *(R)*	3.50	12.00
#121 Harold Carmichael *(R)*	3.00	10.00
#150 John Unitas	3.50	12.00
#220 Franco Harris	6.00	20.00
#383 John Hannah *(R)*	3.00	10.00
#500 Roger Staubach	4.50	18.00
1975 Topps		
Complete Set (528)	75.00	300.00
Common Player	.15	.30
#12 Mel Blount *(R)*	3.00	10.00
#145 Roger Staubach	4.00	15.00
#282 Lynn Swann *(R)*	8.00	25.00
#367 Dan Fouts *(R)*	13.00	50.00
#416 Joe Theismann *(R)*	4.00	15.00
#500 O. J. Simpson	3.00	10.00
1976 Topps		
Complete Set (528)	90.00	350.00
Common Player	.15	.30
#128 Dan Fouts	6.00	23.00
#148 Walter Payton *(R)*	50.00	190.00
#158 Randy White *(R)*	6.00	18.00
#220 Jack Lambert *(R)*	8.00	30.00
#300 O. J. Simpson	3.00	10.00
#376 Steve Grogan *(R)*	1.80	5.00
#480 Mel Blount	1.00	4.00
#500 Fran Tarkenton	2.00	8.00
#516 Brian Sipe *(R)*	1.00	4.00
1977 Topps		
Complete Set (528)	60.00	280.00
Common Player	.10	.20
#18 Pat Haden *(R)*	1.00	3.00
#45 Roger Staubach	2.00	8.00
#99 Marvin Webster *(R)*	1.50	6.00
#100 O. J. Simpson	2.00	8.00
#177 Steve Largent *(R)*	15.00	60.00
#274 Dan Fouts	2.00	8.00

Cards (listed by year and maker)	Very Good	Near Mint
1977 Topps (*Continued*)		
#360 Walter Payton	10.00	40.00
#467 Chuck Muncie *(R)*	.75	3.00
#515 Bob Griese	1.00	4.00
1978 Topps		
Complete Set (528)	40.00	135.00
Common Player	.05	.10
#65 Terry Bradshaw	1.00	4.00
#100 Fran Tarkenton	1.25	5.00
#200 Walter Payton	6.00	22.00
#315 Tony Dorsett *(R)*	14.00	52.00
#320 John Stallworth *(R)*	8.00	23.00
#361 Stanley Morgan *(R)*	1.50	5.00
#400 O. J. Simpson	2.00	8.00
#443 Steve Largent	4.00	15.00
#500 Franco Harris	2.50	7.00
1979 Topps		
Complete Set (528)	30.00	100.00
Common Player	.05	.10
#77 Steve DeBerg *(R)*	1.50	6.00
#160 Tony Dorsett	2.00	7.00
#308 Ozzie Newsome *(R)*	8.00	30.00
#310 James Lofton *(R)*	13.00	48.00
#389 Ed O'Neil *(R)*	4.00	15.00
#390 Earl Campbell *(R)*	8.00	35.00
#400 Roger Staubach	3.00	10.00
#480 Walter Payton	1.50	5.00
#500 Terry Bradshaw	1.25	4.00
1980 Topps		
Complete Set (528)	20.00	80.00
Common Player	.05	.10
#1 Ottis Anderson *(R)*	1.50	5.00
#78 James Lofton	3.30	12.00
#160 Walter Payton	3.00	10.00
#225 Phil Simms *(R)*	8.00	20.00
#330 Tony Dorsett	1.00	4.00
1981 Topps		
Complete Set (528)	80.00	300.00

Cards (listed by year and maker)	Very Good	Near Mint
1981 Topps (*Continued*)		
Common Player	.10	.20
#11 Vince Evans (R)	.75	3.00
#150 Kellen Winslow (R)	3.00	10.00
#100 Billy Sims (R)	.45	1.50
#194 Art Monk (R)	13.00	48.00
#216 Joe Montana (R)	65.00	250.00
#271 Steve Largent	2.00	8.00
#316 Dan Hampton (R)	3.00	12.00
#500 Tony Dorsett	.80	3.00
1982 Topps		
Complete Set (528)	25.00	100.00
Common Player	.05	.10
#51 Anthony Munoz (R)	1.80	7.50
#176 Freeman McNeil (R)	1.00	4.00
#204 Terry Bradshaw	.75	2.00
#226 James Brooks (R)	1.60	6.00
#249 Steve Largent	1.00	3.50
#302 Walter Payton	1.00	4.00
#311 Tony Dorsett	.75	2.00
#410 George Rogers (R)	.50	1.25
#433 Phil Simms	2.50	7.00
#434 Lawrence Taylor (R)	10.00	38.00
#471 Neil Lomax (R)	.50	1.00
#486 Ronnie Lott (R)	9.00	26.00
#488 Joe Montana	10.00	30.00
1983 Topps		
Complete Set (396)	22.00	75.00
Common Player	.05	.10
#33 Jim McMahon (R)	.50	2.00
#36 Walter Payton	.70	3.00
#38 Mike Singletary (R)	2.50	10.00
#46 Tony Dorsett	.25	1.00
#133 Lawrence Taylor	1.70	9.00
#156 Roy Green (R)	.50	2.00
#169 Joe Montana	2.25	11.00
#193 Art Monk	.50	2.00
#294 Marcus Allen (R)	2.50	13.00
#374 Dan Fouts	.70	3.00
#389 Steve Largent	.60	2.50

Cards (listed by year and maker)	**Very Good**	**Near Mint**
1984 Topps		
Complete Set (396)	30.00	110.00
Common Player	.08	.24
#63 John Elway (R)	5.00	18.00
#98 Marcus Allen	.50	2.00
#111 Howie Long (R)	.60	2.50
#123 Dan Marino (R)	11.00	46.00
#165 Franco Harris	.85	3.00
#179 Dan Fouts	.25	1.00
#195 Dave Krieg (R)	.70	2.75
#280 Eric Dickerson (R)	5.00	20.00
#353 Roger Craig (R)	2.00	8.50
#358 Joe Montana	2.00	10.00
#380 Darrell Green (R)	1.50	7.00
1984 Topps USFL		
Complete Set (132)	130.00	590.00
Common Player	.20	.80
#1 Luther Bradley	.30	1.50
#3 Trumaine Johnson (R)	.30	1.50
#4 Greg Landry	.25	1.00
#14 Scott Norwood (R)	.50	2.00
#16 Cliff Stoudt (R)	.25	1.00
#17 Vince Evans	.25	1.00
#34 Sam Harrell (R)	.30	1.50
#36 Jim Kelley (R)	45.00	210.00
#38 Rickey Sanders (R)	3.00	12.00
#42 Vaughan Johnson (R)	5.00	20.00
#52 Steve Young (R)	50.00	220.00
#58 Reggie White (R)	12.00	50.00
#62 Bobby Hebert (R)	8.00	32.00
#74 Herschel Walker (R)	25.00	90.00
#96 Doug Williams	1.00	4.00
#114 Gary Anderson (R)	1.00	4.00
1985 Topps		
Complete Set (396)	20.00	80.00
Common Player	.05	.10
#24 Richard Dent (R)	.80	3.75
#33 Walter Payton	.35	1.50
#34 Mike Singletary	.40	1.75
#79 Eric Dickerson	.75	3.50
#80 Henry Ellard (R)	.75	3.00

Cards (listed by year and maker)	Very Good	Near Mint
1985 Topps (*Continued*)		
#157 Joe Montana	1.00	4.00
#238 John Elway	.75	3.50
#251 Warren Moon (*R*)	5.50	30.00
#308 Mark Clayton (*R*)	1.25	5.00
#358 Louis Lipps (*R*)	.75	3.50
#372 Dan Fouts	.25	.80
#389 Steve Largent	.30	1.00
1985 Topps USFL		
Complete Set (132)	30.00	150.00
Common Player	.35	1.50
#8 Doug Williams	1.00	4.00
#19 Sam Mills (*R*)	1.25	5.00
#45 Jim Kelly	15.00	60.00
#49 Gary Clark (*R*)	25.00	75.00
#65 Steve Young	30.00	100.00
#80 Doug Flutie (*R*)	5.00	20.00
#86 Herschel Walker	5.00	20.00
#92 Anthony Carter	3.50	12.00
1986 Topps		
Complete Set (396)	25.00	100.00
Common Player	.05	.10
#11 Walter Payton	.30	1.50
#20 William Perry (*R*)	.25	1.00
#25 Wilbur Marshall (*R*)	.30	1.50
#45 Dan Marino	.75	5.00
#101 Al Toon (*R*)	.30	1.50
#112 John Elway	.50	2.00
#148 Leonard Marshall (*R*)	.25	1.00
#156 Joe Montana	.75	3.00
#161 Jerry Rice (*R*)	15.00	45.00
#176 Gary Clark (*R*)	1.50	6.00
#187 Bernie Kosar (*R*)	1.50	6.00
#255 Boomer Esiason (*R*)	2.00	8.50
#275 Reggie White	1.50	6.00
#350 Warren Moon	1.00	4.00
#374 Steve Young	.75	3.00
#388 Andre Reed (*R*)	2.00	8.00
1987 Topps		
Complete Set (396)	12.50	50.00
Common Player	.05	.10

Cards (listed by year and maker)	Very Good	Near Mint
1987 Topps (*Continued*)		
#31 John Elway	.10	.50
#46 Walter Payton	.25	1.00
#112 Joe Montana	.50	2.00
#115 Jerry Rice	2.00	8.00
#145 Jim Everett (*R*)	2.00	8.00
#264 Herschel Walker	.50	2.00
#296 Randall Cunningham (*R*)	3.50	15.00
#340 Dan Fouts	.50	2.00
#362 Jim Kelly	3.00	11.00
#384 Steve Young	1.00	4.00
1988 Topps		
Complete Set (396)	8.00	25.00
Common Player	.05	.10
#14 Ricky Sanders (*R*)	.25	1.00
#71 Neal Anderson (*R*)	1.50	6.00
#103 Warren Moon	.90	4.00
#190 Dan Marino	1.00	4.00
#230 Cornelius Bennett (*R*)	.75	3.00
#327 Bo Jackson (*R*)	1.00	4.00
#221 Jim Kelly	.50	2.00
#328 Marcus Allen	.75	3.00
#363 Christian Okoye (*R*)	.75	3.00
1989 Action Packed		
Complete Set (30)	10.00	35.00
Common Player	.30	1.50
#1 Neal Anderson	.50	2.00
#9 Mike Singletary	.75	3.00
#17 Dave Meggett (*R*)	1.00	4.00
#20 Lawrence Taylor	1.00	4.00
#26 Art Monk	.75	3.00
#29 Mark Rypien (*R*)	5.00	20.00
1989 Pro Set		
Complete Set (540)	9.00	35.00
Common Player	.05	.15
#32 Thurman Thomas (*R*)	.75	3.00
#47 William Perry	1.25	5.00
#100 John Elway	1.25	5.00
#185 Bo Jackson	.50	2.00
#404 Curt Warner	2.00	8.00

Cards (listed by year and maker)	Very Good	Near Mint
1989 Pro Set (*Continued*)		
#434 Mark Rypien (*R*)	.50	2.00
#494 Barry Sanders (*R*)	2.00	8.00
#535 Gizmo Williams (*R*)	5.00	20.00
1989 Score		
Complete Set (330)	50.00	200.00
Common Player	.15	.30
#1 Joe Montana	.50	2.00
#18 Michael Irvin (*R*)	3.00	11.00
#60 Chris Miller (*R*)	2.00	7.50
#105 Mark Rypien (*R*)	4.00	16.00
#211 Thurman Thomas (*R*)	10.00	40.00
#238 John Taylor (*R*)	1.00	4.00
#246 Deion Sanders (*R*)	2.00	8.00
#257 Barry Sanders (*R*)	10.00	40.00
#270 Troy Aikman (*R*)	10.00	40.00
#272 Andre Rison (*R*)	2.00	8.00
#317 Herschel Walker	1.00	4.00
1989 Topps		
Complete Set (396)	2.00	10.00
Common Player	.01	.04
#45 Thurman Thomas (*R*)	1.00	4.00
#148 Michael Dean Perry (*R*)	.30	1.50
#253 Mark Rypien (*R*)	1.00	4.00
#293 Dan Marino	.30	1.50
#341 Chris Miller (*R*)	.75	3.00
#353 Christian Okoye (*R*)	.30	1.50
#379 Sterling Sharpe (*R*)	.50	2.00
1990 Action Packed		
Complete Set (281)	20.00	80.00
Common Player	.20	.40
#9 Deion Sanders	.50	2.00
#20 Thurman Thomas	.50	2.00
#51 Troy Aikman	.75	3.00
#78 Barry Sanders	1.50	6.00
#97 Warren Moon	.50	2.00
#146 Dan Marino	.75	3.00
#246 Joe Montana	.85	4.00
#248 Jerry Rice	.50	2.00
#258 Paul Skansi (*R*)	.50	2.00
#XX Jim Plunkett braille	2.50	10.00

Cards (listed by year and maker)	**Very Good**	**Near Mint**
1990 Fleer		
Complete Set (400)	3.00	10.00
Common Player	.03	.06
#10A Joe Montana	1.00	4.00
#10B Joe Montana	.50	2.00
#284 Barry Sanders	1.00	4.00
#347 Jeff George (R)	.50	2.00
#370 Blair Thomas (R)	.30	1.25
1990 Pro Set		
Complete Set (800)	8.00	25.00
Common Player	.05	.10
#75 Cody Risien	2.50	10.00
#161 Art Shell	.50	2.00
#289 Charles Haley	.50	2.00
#338 Eric Dickerson	2.00	10.00
#685 Emmitt Smith	.75	3.00
#711 Carwell Gardner (R)	.50	2.00
1990 Score		
Complete Set (665)	3.00	12.00
Common Player	.02	.05
#20 Barry Sanders	.20	.80
#110 Thurman Thomas	.25	1.00
#232 Jim Harbaugh (R)	.20	.80
#307 Rodney Hampton	.25	1.00
#309 John Friesz (R)	.15	.60
#398 Heath Sherman (R)	.15	.60
#506 Haywood Jeffires (R)	.10	.40
#607 Andre Ware (R)	.10	.40
#634 Jeff George (R)	.25	1.00
#651 Scott Mitchell (R)	.15	.60
1990 Topps		
Complete Set (528)	2.50	10.00
Common Player	.02	.05
#6 Dexter Carter (R)	.10	.40
#13 Joe Montana	.15	.50
#93 Randall Cunningham	.10	.40
#174 Barry Foster (R)	.50	2.00
#206 Thurman Thomas	.10	.40
#225 Haywood Jeffires (R)	.50	1.90
#289 Marcus Allen	.15	.45

Cards (listed by year and maker)	Very Good	Near Mint
1990 Topps (*Continued*)		
#298 Jeff George (R)	.20	.80
#352 Barry Sanders	.20	.80
#448 Blair Thomas (R)	.10	.40
#471 Michael Haynes (R)	.15	.45
#482 Troy Aikman	.25	1.00
1991 Action Packed		
Complete Set (291)	16.00	60.00
Common Player	.15	.35
#3 Brian Jordan	.25	1.00
#20 Thurman Thomas	.50	2.00
#78 Barry Sanders	.65	3.00
#124 Bo Jackson	.25	1.00
#197 Rob Moore	2.00	8.50
#204 Randall Cunningham	.50	2.00
#247 Joe Montana	.65	3.00
#248 Jerry Rice	.65	2.00
1991 Bowman		
Complete Set (561)	2.50	10.00
Common Player	.02	.05
#71 Chris Zorich (R)	.10	.40
#117 Emmitt Smith	.25	1.00
#253 Todd Marinovich (R)	.20	.80
#285 Dan Marino	.10	.40
#376 Browning Nagle (R)	.20	.80
#489 Ricky Watters (R)	.20	1.00
#528 Ricky Ervins (R)	.20	.80
1991 Classic		
Complete Set (50)	4.50	16.00
Common Player	.10	.25
#1 Raghib Ismail (R)	1.25	4.50
#2 Russell Maryland (R)	.75	2.00
#11 Alvin Harper (R)	.75	2.00
#30 Brett Favre (R)	1.10	4.00
1991 Fleer		
Complete Set (432)	3.00	12.00
Common Player	.02	.05
#70 Warren Moon	.10	.40
#237 Emmitt Smith	.50	2.00

Cards (listed by year and maker)	Very Good	Near Mint
1991 Fleer (*Continued*)		
#408 Joe Montana	.15	.45
#423 Russell Maryland (*R*)	.10	.40
1991 Fleer Ultra		
Complete Set (300)	4.00	14.00
Common Player	.06	.20
#59 Jeff George	.30	.90
#162 Troy Aikman	.50	2.00
#165 Emmitt Smith	.50	2.00
#169 Barry Sanders	.50	2.00
#251 Joe Montana	.50	2.00
#265 Steve Young	.30	1.25
#283 Brett Favre (*R*)	.75	3.00
#298 Chris Zorich (*R*)	.50	2.00
1991 Pacific		
Complete Set (660)	6.00	22.00
Common Player	.05	.10
#93 Troy Aikman	.25	1.00
#107 Emmitt Smith	.25	1.00
#144 Barry Sanders	.30	1.50
#541 Chris Zorich (*R*)	.25	1.00
#551 Brett Favre (*R*)	.50	2.00
#623 Browning Nagle (*R*)	.30	1.50
#659 Ricky Ervins (*R*)	.20	.80
1991 Pro Set		
Complete Set (850)	8.00	32.00
Common Player	.05	.10
#1 Emmitt Smith	.30	1.25
#3 Joe Montana	.25	1.00
#36 Raghib Ismail	.75	3.00
#37 Ty Detmer	.25	1.00
#92 Darion Connor	.50	2.00
#175 Eric Dickerson	.25	1.00
#388 Barry Sanders	.25	1.00
#485 Emmitt Smith	.30	1.50
#694 Russell Maryland	.50	2.00
#762 Brett Favre (*R*)	.50	2.00
#844 Barry Foster (*R*)	.50	2.00
#845 Neil O'Donnell (*R*)	.50	2.00

Cards (listed by year and maker)	Very Good	Near Mint

1991 Pro Set Platinum

		Very Good	Near Mint
Complete Set (315)		4.00	15.00
Common Player		.05	.10
#24	Troy Aikman	.35	1.75
#25	Emmitt Smith	.50	2.00
#33	Barry Sanders	.30	1.50
#258	Barry Foster	.25	1.00
#289	Ricky Ervins (R)	.30	1.50
#290	Brett Favre (R)	.35	1.75

1991 Pro Set World League

		Very Good	Near Mint
Complete Set (150)		2.50	10.00
Common Player		.02	.05
#35	Scott Erney (R)	.20	.75
#39	Tony Rice (R)	.20	.75
#80	Stan Gelbaugh	.25	1.00
#131	Roman Gabriel	.25	1.00
#137	Carl Parker (R)	.15	.50

1991 Score

		Very Good	Near Mint
Complete Set (686)		2.50	10.00
Common Player		.01	.03
#15	Emmitt Smith	.20	.80
#225	Troy Aikman	.15	.50
#568	Herman Moore (R)	.25	1.00
#569	Bill Musgrave (R)	.15	.50
#575	Ricky Watters (R)	.50	2.00
#611	Brett Favre (R)	.35	1.75

1991 Score Pinnacle

		Very Good	Near Mint
Complete Set (415)		13.00	50.00
Common Player		.05	.10
#1	Warren Moon	.35	1.50
#6	Troy Aikman	.35	1.50
#42	Emmitt Smith	1.50	5.50
#66	Joe Montana	1.00	4.00
#250	Barry Sanders	.80	3.50
#300	Ricky Ervins (R)	.90	4.00
#336	Leonard Russell (R)	.75	3.00

1991 Star Pics

	Very Good	Near Mint
Complete Set (112)	2.50	10.00
Common Player	.02	.05

Cards (listed by year and maker)	Very Good	Near Mint
1991 Star Pics		
#74 Bill Musgrave (R)	.20	.80
#97 Darryl Lewis (R)	.15	.60
#107 Alvin Harper (R)	.90	3.50
1991 Topps		
Complete Set (660)	2.00	8.00
Common Player	.01	.02
#83 Todd Marinovich (R)	.10	.40
#266 Dan McGwire (R)	.10	.40
#360 Emmitt Smith	.20	.80
#415 Barry Sanders	.10	.40
#554 John Elway	.10	.40
1991 Topps Stadium Club		
Complete Set (500)	40.00	150.00
Common Player	.10	.40
#2 Emmitt Smith	4.50	18.00
#71 Jerry Rice	.75	3.00
#228 Troy Aikman	2.00	7.50
#290 Chris Zorich (R)	.75	3.00
#353 Ricky Ervins (R)	2.00	10.00
#361 Barry Sanders (R)	2.00	10.00
#395 Thurman Thomas	2.00	8.00
#417 Andre Reed	1.00	4.00
1991 Upper Deck		
Complete Set (700)	4.00	15.00
Common Player	.02	.05
#4 Mike Croel (R)	.25	1.00
#7 Dan McGwire (R)	.20	.80
#9 Ricky Watters (R)	.30	1.25
#11 Browning Nagle (R)	.30	1.25
#13 Brett Favre (R)	.30	1.25
#54 Joe Montana	.25	1.00
#83 Dan Marino	.15	.60
#152 Troy Aikman	.25	1.00
#172 Emmitt Smith	.75	3.00
#356 Thurman Thomas	.15	.60
#444 Barry Sanders	.50	2.00
#622 Leonard Russell (R)	.25	1.00
#640 Ricky Ervins (R)	.30	1.40

Cards (listed by year and maker)	Very Good	Near Mint
1991 Wild Card		
Complete Set (160)	5.00	20.00
Common Player	.03	.06
#46 Emmitt Smith	1.00	3.50
#89 Barry Sanders	.75	2.75
#118 Ricky Ervins (R)	.25	1.00
#126 Surprise Card	.50	2.00
#135 Thurman Thomas	.20	.80
1992 Action Packed		
Complete Set (288)	20.00	70.00
Common Player	.15	.30
#15 Thurman Thomas	.30	1.25
#56 Emmitt Smith	2.00	8.00
#72 Barry Sanders	.50	2.00
#222 Barry Foster	.50	2.00
#283 Emmitt Smith braille	3.00	12.00
1992 Bowman		
Complete Set (573)	70.00	270.00
Common Player	.10	.25
#13 Michael Irvin	.50	2.00
#20 Sterling Sharpe	.20	.80
#46 Neil O'Donnell	.25	1.00
#100 Emmitt Smith	15.75	60.00
#112 Thurman Thomas	1.00	4.00
#170 Barry Sanders	1.00	4.00
#180 Emmitt Smith	42.00	160.00
#221 Barry Sanders	1.50	6.00
#246 Steve Young	.50	2.00
#349 Art Monk	.50	2.00
#409 Barry Foster	1.00	4.00
#469 Reggie White	.25	1.00
#505 Andre Rison	.20	.80
1992 Classic		
Complete Set (100)	2.00	10.00
Common Player	.05	.10
#1 Desmond Howard	.25	1.00
#2 David Klingler	.20	.80
#36 Mike Pawlawski	.15	.60
#58 Tommy Maddox	.15	.60

Cards (listed by year and maker)	Very Good	Near Mint
1992 Collector's Edge		
Complete Set (175)	20.00	80.00
Common Player	.07	.15
#7 Jim Kelly	1.00	4.00
#11 Thurman Thomas	.75	3.00
#31 Troy Aikman	2.00	8.00
#32 Emmitt Smith	2.50	10.00
#33 Michael Irvin	1.00	4.00
#56 Warren Moon	.50	2.00
#90 Dan Marino	.50	2.00
#145 Neil O'Donnell	1.00	4.00
#156 Jerry Rice	1.25	5.00
#170 Mark Rypien	1.00	4.00
1992 Courtside		
Complete Set (140)	4.00	15.00
Common Player	.05	.10
#1 Steve Emtman	.20	.80
#28 Tracy Scroggins	.10	.40
#25 Ty Detmer	.50	2.00
#50 Tommy Vardell	.20	.80
#71 Matt Rodgers	.10	.40
#87 T. J. Rubley	.10	.40
#104 Santana Dotson	.15	.60
#111 Marquez Pope	.10	.40
1992 Fleer		
Complete Set (480)	2.50	10.00
Common Player	.03	.06
#15 Andre Rison	.20	.80
#80 Alvin Harper	.15	.60
#371 Steve Bono (*R*)	.25	1.00
#386 Steve Young	.20	.80
#440 Matt LaBounty (*R*)	.10	.35
#441 Amp Lee (*R*)	.20	.80
#475 Emmitt Smith	.25	1.00
1992 Fleer Ultra		
Complete Set (450)	7.50	30.00
Common Player	.05	.10
#31 Thurman Thomas	.25	1.00
#88 Emmitt Smith	1.50	6.00
#122 Barry Sanders	1.00	4.00

Cards (listed by year and maker)	Very Good	Near Mint
1992 Fleer Ultra (*Continued*)		
#331 Barry Foster	.50	2.00
#357 Steve Bono (*R*)	.50	2.00
#433 Amp Lee (*R*)	.75	3.00
#444 Tommy Vardell (*R*)	.50	2.00
1992 GameDay		
Complete Set (500)	20.00	75.00
Common Player	.10	.20
#4 Ricky Ervins	.25	1.00
#48 David Klingler (*R*)	.75	3.00
#82 Steve Emtman (*R*)	.50	2.00
#141 Steve Bono (*R*)	.50	2.00
#244 Tommy Maddox (*R*)	.35	1.25
#261 Browning Nagle (*R*)	.50	2.00
#439 Tommy Vardell (*R*)	.25	1.00
#490 Emmitt Smith	1.00	4.00
#496 Nick Bell (*R*)	.20	.80
1992 Pacific		
Complete Set (660)	5.00	22.00
Common Player	.03	.05
#68 Emmitt Smith	.25	1.00
#259 Neil O'Donnell	.20	.80
#320 Amp Lee (*R*)	.10	.50
#652 Tony Smith (*R*)	.20	.80
1992 Playoff		
Complete Set (150)	15.00	60.00
Common Player	.10	.20
#1 Emmitt Smith	2.50	12.00
#42 Steve Bono	.50	2.00
#68 Barry Foster	.50	2.00
#138 Barry Sanders	.75	3.25
#150 Ricky Watters	1.00	4.00
1992 Pro Set		
Complete Set (700)	3.50	15.00
Common Player	.03	.05
#28 Terrell Buckley (*R*)	.20	.80
#29 Amp Lee (*R*)	.15	.60
#150 Emmitt Smith	.25	1.00

Cards (listed by year and maker)	Very Good	Near Mint
1992 Pro Set (*Continued*)		
#459 David Klingler (*R*)	.20	.80
#486 Tommy Maddox (*R*)	.20	.80
#649 Joe Montana	.10	.40
1992 Score		
Complete Set (550)	2.00	8.00
Common Player	.01	.02
#1 Barry Sanders	.10	.40
#65 Emmitt Smith	.12	.50
#313 Steve Bono	.05	.20
#493 Tommy Vardell (*R*)	.10	.50
#494 Terrell Buckley (*R*)	.10	.40
1992 Score Pinnacle		
Complete Set (360)	10.00	35.00
Common Player	.05	.10
#15 Barry Sanders	.75	3.00
#58 Emmitt Smith	1.50	6.50
#121 Barry Foster	.50	2.00
#178 Neil O'Donnell	.25	1.00
#303 Brett Favre	.50	2.00
#316 Amp Lee (*R*)	.25	1.00
#360 Terrell Buckley (*R*)	.30	1.50
1992 SkyBox Impact		
Complete Set (350)	5.00	20.00
Common Player	.04	.08
#232 Troy Aikman	.25	1.00
#275 Emmitt Smith	.80	3.50
#321 Steve Emtman (*R*)	.25	1.00
#322 Carl Pickens (*R*)	.25	1.00
#323 David Klingler (*R*)	.25	1.00
#336 Tommy Maddox (*R*)	.25	1.00
#350 Edgar Bennett (*R*)	.75	3.00
1992 SkyBox PrimeTime		
Complete Set (350)	10.00	40.00
Common Player	.12	.25
#16 Joe Montana	.25	1.00
#22 Emmitt Smith	1.00	4.00
#156 Steve Emtman (*R*)	.50	2.00

Cards (listed by year and maker)	Very Good	Near Mint
1992 SkyBox PrimeTime (*Continued*)		
#165 Emmitt Smith	.50	2.00
#166 Tommy Maddox	.50	2.00
#238 David Klingler (*R*)	.75	3.00
#313 Troy Aikman	.25	1.00
#339 Alvin Harper	.25	1.00
1992 Star Pics		
Complete Set (113)	3.00	12.00
Common Player	.02	.04
#12 Tommy Vardell	.20	.80
#23 Quentin Coryatt	.10	.40
#26 Vaughan Dunbar	.20	.80
#50 Leonard Russell	.10	.40
#51 Matt Rodgers	.10	.40
#60 Carl Pickens	.20	.75
#70 Thurman Thomas	.20	.80
#90 Steve Emtman	.25	1.00
1992 Topps		
Complete Set (759)	7.50	30.00
Common Player	.02	.05
#180 Emmitt Smith	.30	1.50
#250 Amp Lee (*R*)	.25	1.00
#665 Jerry Rice	.50	2.00
#682 Dan Marino	.20	.80
#686 Tommy Maddox (*R*)	.75	3.00
#694 David Klingler (*R*)	.60	2.50
#742 Steve Emtman (*R*)	.50	2.00
#744 Troy Aikman	1.00	4.00
1992 Topps Stadium Club		
Complete Set (600)	12.00	45.00
Common Player	.05	.15
#38 Barry Sanders	.50	2.00
#134 Thurman Thomas	.40	1.60
#190 Emmitt Smith	1.00	4.00
#301 Barry Sanders	.75	3.00
#303 Emmitt Smith	1.50	6.00
#380 Barry Foster	.75	3.00
#419 Tommy Vardell (*R*)	.25	1.00
#447 Michael Irvin	.25	1.00
#583 Amp Lee (*R*)	.25	1.00

Cards (listed by year and maker)	Very Good	Near Mint
1992 Ultimate World League		
Complete Set (200)	6.00	25.00
Common Player	.03	.05
#50 Mike Perez	.10	.40
#105 Anthony Parker	.10	.40
#127 Scott Mitchell	.25	1.00
#144 David Archer	.25	1.00
#174 Amir Rasul (R)	.25	1.00
1992 Upper Deck		
Complete Set (700)	6.00	25.00
Common Player	.03	.05
#9 Ricky Watters (R)	.50	2.00
#172 Emmitt Smith	.75	3.00
#444 Barry Sanders	.50	2.00
#640 Ricky Ervins (R)	.25	1.00
1992 Wild Card		
Complete Set (460)	7.00	28.00
Common Player	.04	.08
#1 Surprise Card	.50	2.00
#161 Emmitt Smith	.50	2.00
#273 Emmitt Smith	.40	1.50
#354 Tommy Maddox (R)	.25	1.00
#391 Barry Foster	.30	1.50
1992 Wild Card World League		
Complete Set (150)	7.50	30.00
Common Player	.05	.10
#50 David Archer	.30	1.50
#58 Darryl Clack	.25	1.00
#67 Scott Mitchell	.50	2.00
#73 Reggie Slack (R)	.50	2.00
1993 Action Packed		
Complete Set (162)	10.00	40.00
Common Player	.05	.20
#11 Troy Aikman	1.00	4.00
#13 Emmitt Smith	1.25	5.00
#23 Joe Montana	.75	3.00
#26 Dan Marino	.50	2.00

Cards (listed by year and maker)	Very Good	Near Mint
1993 Bowman		
Complete Set (423)	15.00	60.00
Common Player	.05	.10
#1 Troy Aikman	1.25	5.00
#50 Rick Mirer (R)	2.00	8.00
#200 Joe Montana	1.25	5.00
#264 Jerome Bettis (R)	2.25	7.00
#280 Drew Bledsoe (R)	1.75	6.25
#300 Emmitt Smith	2.00	8.00
1993 Collector's Edge		
Complete Set (250)	8.00	32.00
Common Player	.03	.06
#44 Troy Aikman	1.00	4.00
#48 Emmitt Smith	1.25	5.00
#64 Barry Sanders	.50	2.00
#223 Jerry Rice	.50	2.00
1993 Fleer		
Complete Set (500)	5.00	20.00
Common Player	.01	.04
#103 Brett Favre	.25	1.00
#223 Emmitt Smith	.60	2.50
#275 Troy Aikman	.50	2.00
1993 Fleer Ultra		
Complete Set (500)	8.50	34.00
Common Player	.03	.06
#41 Curtis Conway (R)	.50	2.00
#101 Emmitt Smith	1.00	4.00
#135 Barry Sanders	.25	1.00
#203 Joe Montana	.75	3.00
#232 Jerome Bettis (R)	1.00	4.00
#259 O. J. McDuffie (R)	.30	1.25
#283 Drew Bledsoe (R)	1.00	4.00
#416 Natrone Means (R)	.30	1.25
#437 Jerry Rice	.50	2.00
#456 Rick Mirer (R)	1.00	4.00
1993 GameDay		
Complete Set (500)	10.00	40.00
Common Player	.05	.10
#11 Drew Bledsoe (R)	2.00	8.00

Cards (listed by year and maker)	**Very Good**	**Near Mint**
1993 GameDay (*Continued*)		
#22 Emmitt Smith	1.00	4.00
#36 Joe Montana	.50	2.00
#339 Jerome Bettis (*R*)	1.50	6.00
#402 Rick Mirer (*R*)	1.25	5.00
1993 Pacific		
Complete Set (440)	4.00	16.00
Common Player	.01	.02
#1 Emmitt Smith	.25	1.00
#106 Barry Sanders	.20	.80
#385 Rick Mirer (*R*)	.75	3.00
1993 Pinnacle		
Complete Set (360)	7.50	28.00
Common Player	.02	.04
#1 Brett Favre	.25	1.00
#100 Emmitt Smith	.75	3.00
#138 Thurman Thomas	.30	1.25
#277 Joe Montana	.50	2.00
#281 Troy Aikman	.60	2.50
1993 Playoff		
Complete Set (315)	18.00	75.00
Common Player	.07	.15
#1 Troy Aikman	1.00	4.00
#10 Emmitt Smith	2.00	8.00
#198 Sterling Sharpe	.75	3.00
#217 Barry Sanders	.60	2.50
#294 Jerome Bettis (*R*)	2.50	10.00
#295 Drew Bledsoe (*R*)	2.00	8.00
#308 Rick Mirer (*R*)	1.80	8.50
1993 Pro Set		
Complete Set (449)	4.50	18.00
Common Player	.01	.02
#7 Emmitt Smith	.50	2.00
#30 Troy Aikman	.50	2.00
#125 Glyn Milburn (*R*)	.20	.80
#226 Jerome Bettis (*R*)	.75	3.00
#270 Drew Bledsoe (*R*)	.75	3.00
#380 Natrone Means (*R*)	.50	2.00
#411 Rick Mirer (*R*)	.75	3.00

Cards (listed by year and maker)	Very Good	Near Mint
1993 Pro Set Power		
Complete Set (200)	2.00	8.00
Common Player	.01	.02
#8 Troy Aikman	.25	1.00
#22 Emmitt Smith	.25	1.00
#200 Joe Montana	.25	1.00
1993 Score		
Complete Set (440)	2.00	8.00
Common Player	.01	.02
#14 Emmitt Smith	.20	.75
#25 Brett Favre	.20	.80
#238 Troy Aikman	.20	.80
#253 Joe Montana	.25	1.00
#306 Jerome Bettis (R)	.25	1.00
1993 SkyBox NFL		
Complete Set (270)	8.00	32.00
Common Player	.03	.06
#7 Drew Bledsoe (R)	1.50	6.00
#10 Troy Aikman	.75	3.00
#64 Emmitt Smith	1.00	4.00
#183 Natrone Means (R)	.40	1.50
#223 O. J. McDuffie (R)	.50	2.00
1993 Topps Stadium Club		
Complete Set (550)	12.50	52.00
Common Player	.05	.10
#50 Troy Aikman	.50	2.00
#85 Emmitt Smith	.75	3.00
#108 Jerome Bettis (R)	1.50	6.00
#180 Rick Mirer (R)	1.50	6.00
#280 Drew Bledsoe (R)	1.50	6.00
#440 Joe Montana	.50	2.00
1993 Upper Deck		
Complete Set (530)	8.00	27.00
Common Player	.03	.06
#3 Rick Mirer (R)	.75	3.00
#11 Drew Bledsoe (R)	.75	3.00
#20 Jerome Bettis (R)	.50	2.00
#140 Troy Aikman	.25	1.00
#350 Emmitt Smith	.30	1.20

Cards (listed by year and maker)	Very Good	Near Mint
1993 Upper Deck (*Continued*)		
#454 Barry Sanders	.20	.80
#460 Joe Montana	.25	1.00
#479 Natrone Means (*R*)	.25	1.00
1993 Upper Deck SP		
Complete Set (270)	10.00	40.00
Common Player	.07	.15
#6 Jerome Bettis (*R*)	1.00	4.00
#9 Drew Bledsoe (*R*)	1.25	5.00
#16 Rick Mirer (*R*)	1.25	5.00
#64 Troy Aikman	1.50	6.00
#72 Emmitt Smith	1.75	7.50
#122 Joe Montana	.75	3.00
#150 Dan Marino	.50	2.00
#151 Scott Mitchell	.40	1.60
#240 Jerry Rice	.30	1.25
#242 Ricky Watters	.30	1.25
1993 Wild Card		
Complete Set (200)	2.00	8.00
Common Player	.01	.02
#1 Surprise Card	.25	1.00
#39 Glyn Milburn (*R*)	.20	.80
#67 Joe Montana	.20	.80
#86 Troy Aikman	.20	.80
#87 Emmitt Smith	.30	1.50
#141 Drew Bledsoe (*R*)	.25	1.00
#159 Jerome Bettis (*R*)	.20	.80
#179 Rick Mirer (*R*)	.20	.80
1994 Action Packed		
Complete Set (120)	15.00	35.00
Common Player	.05	.10
#20 Troy Aikman	1.00	4.00
#22 Emmitt Smith	1.00	4.00
#70 Drew Bledsoe	.75	3.00
#106 Jerry Rice	.30	1.50
#108 Steve Young	.25	1.00
#111 Rick Mirer	.75	3.00
Catching Fire (10)	3.00	12.00
#1 Jerry Rice	.50	2.00
#3 Michael Irvin	.30	1.25

Cards (listed by year and maker)	Very Good	Near Mint

1994 Action Packed (*Continued*)

		Very Good	Near Mint
Fantasy Forecast (42)		6.50	25.00
#4	Emmitt Smith	1.00	4.00
#5	Troy Aikman	1.00	4.00
#6	Jerry Rice	.50	2.00
#8	Jerome Bettis	1.00	4.00
#12	Dan Marino	.60	2.50
#18	Barry Sanders	.50	2.00
#31	Joe Montana	.75	3.00

1994 Classic Pro Line

		Very Good	Near Mint
Complete Set (405)		8.00	25.00
Common Player		.02	.04
#1	Emmitt Smith	.30	1.25
#61	Joe Montana	.25	1.00
#71	Jerome Bettis	.50	2.00
#140	Rick Mirer	.50	2.00
#329	Marshall Faulk (*R*)	1.00	4.00
#330	Heath Shuler (*R*)	1.00	4.00
#348	Johnnie Morton (*R*)	.25	1.00
#355	William Floyd (*R*)	.20	.80
MVP Sweepstakes (45)		50.00	200.00
#5	Troy Aikman	5.00	20.00
#6	Emmitt Smith	4.00	16.00
#36	Steve Young	3.50	14.00
#42	Marshall Faulk	5.00	20.00

1994 Collector's Edge Gold

		Very Good	Near Mint
Complete Set (200)		15.00	60.00
Common Player		.05	.10
#14	Thurman Thomas	.30	1.50
#44	Emmitt Smith	1.00	4.00
#94	Joe Montana	.75	3.00
#127	Drew Bledsoe	1.00	4.00
#175	Natrone Means	.50	2.00
#185	Rick Mirer	1.00	4.00
The Boss Squad (25)		15.00	60.00
#2	Joe Montana	2.00	8.00
#5	Steve Young	1.50	6.00
#13	Emmitt Smith	5.00	20.00
#22	Jerry Rice	2.00	8.00

Cards (listed by year and maker)	Very Good	Near Mint
1994 Fleer		
Complete Set (480)	4.50	18.00
Common Player	.02	.04
#107 Troy Aikman	.25	1.00
#121 Emmitt Smith	.25	1.00
#160 Barry Sanders	.20	.80
#226 Joe Montana	.25	1.00
#252 Jerome Bettis	.50	2.00
#307 Drew Bledsoe	.50	2.00
Scoring Machines (20)	55.00	225.00
#2 Natrone Means	3.00	12.00
#13 Jerry Rice	6.00	25.00
#18 Emmitt Smith	12.00	50.00
#20 Ricky Watters	2.50	10.00
1994 Fleer Ultra		
Complete Set (525)	12.00	48.00
Common Player	.02	.04
#101 Barry Sanders	.25	1.00
#133 Marshall Faulk (*R*)	1.00	4.00
#285 Steve Young	.25	1.00
#498 Deion Sanders	.10	.40
First Rounders (20)	11.00	45.00
#4 Marshall Faulk	3.00	12.00
#14 Johnnie Morton	.60	2.50
1994 GameDay		
Complete Set (420)	8.00	35.00
Common Player	.03	.06
#103 Emmitt Smith	.60	2.50
#179 Marshall Faulk (*R*)	2.00	8.00
#261 Drew Bledsoe	.50	2.00
#368 Jerry Rice	.30	1.50
#414 Heath Shuler (*R*)	.50	2.00
Gamebreakers (16)	7.00	30.00
#1 Troy Aikman	1.00	4.00
#13 Emmitt Smith	1.00	4.00
#16 Steve Young	.25	1.00
1994 Pacific Crown		
Complete Set (450)	7.00	30.00
Common Player	.02	.04
#1 Troy Aikman	.30	1.25

Cards (listed by year and maker)	**Very Good**	**Near Mint**
1994 Pacific Crown (*Continued*)		
#12 Emmitt Smith	.25	1.00
#55 Joe Montana	.25	1.00
#426 Marshall Faulk (*R*)	1.00	4.00
#446 Heath Shuler (*R*)	.75	3.00
Crystaline (20)	25.00	100.00
#1 Emmitt Smith	5.00	20.00
#2 Jerome Bettis	3.00	12.00
#19 Barry Foster	2.00	8.00
1994 Pacific Prisms		
Complete Set (126)	40.00	160.00
Common Player	.25	1.00
#1 Troy Aikman	2.00	8.00
#39 Marshall Faulk (*R*)	5.00	20.00
#72 Natrone Means	2.50	10.00
#85 Johnnie Morton (*R*)	1.00	4.00
#95 Jerry Rice	2.00	8.00
#100 Barry Sanders	2.50	10.00
#110 Emmitt Smith	3.50	15.00
1994 Pinnacle		
Complete Set (271)	5.00	20.00
Common Player	.02	.04
#3 Barry Sanders	.75	3.00
#134 Natrone Means	.50	2.00
#198 Marshall Faulk (*R*)	1.00	4.00
#202 Trent Dilfer (*R*)	.50	2.00
#205 Johnnie Morton (*R*)	.50	2.00
#271 Jerry Rice TD King	1.00	4.00
1994 Playoff		
Complete Set (336)	10.00	40.00
Common Player	.05	.10
#1 Joe Montana	.50	2.00
#25 Troy Aikman	.40	1.50
#132 Rick Mirer	.60	2.50
#150 Steve Young	.25	1.00
#186 Jerry Rice	.50	2.00
#256 Natrone Means	.75	3.00
#304 Marshall Faulk (*R*)	2.00	8.00
#327 William Floyd (*R*)	.25	1.00
#333 Heath Shuler (*R*)	1.00	4.00

Cards (listed by year and maker)	**Very Good**	**Near Mint**
1994 Playoff (*Continued*)		
Rookie Redemption (9)	25.00	110.00
#1 Marshall Faulk	8.00	32.00
#3 Heath Shuler	6.00	24.00
1994 Score		
Complete Set (330)	4.00	16.00
Common Player	.01	.02
#1 Barry Sanders	.25	1.00
#2 Troy Aikman	.25	1.00
#276 Heath Shuler (*R*)	.30	1.50
#277 Marshall Faulk (*R*)	.75	3.00
#330 Emmitt Smith	.25	1.00
Dream Team (18)	50.00	200.00
#1 Troy Aikman	10.00	40.00
#9 Jerry RIce	8.00	32.00
#18 Steve Young	4.00	12.00
1994 SkyBox Impact		
Complete Set (272)	5.00	20.00
Common Player	.02	.04
#63 Emmitt Smith	.50	2.00
#122 Joe Montana	.25	1.00
#166 Drew Bledsoe	.25	1.00
#225 Natrone Means	.50	2.00
1994 SkyBox Premium		
Complete Set (200)	5.00	20.00
Common Player	.02	.05
#41 Emmitt Smith	.40	1.50
#84 Jerome Bettis	.50	2.00
#158 Marshall Faulk (*R*)	.75	3.00
#181 Erict Rhett (*R*)	.50	2.00
Prime Time Rookies (10)	50.00	200.00
#3 Marshall Faulk	20.00	80.00
#7 William Floyd	2.00	8.00
1994 Topps Finest		
Complete Set (220)	50.00	200.00
Common Player	.75	1.50
#1 Emmitt Smith	8.00	32.00
#12 Jerry Rice	2.00	8.00
#41 Rick Mirer (*R*)	5.00	20.00

Cards (listed by year and maker)	**Very Good**	**Near Mint**
1994 Topps Finest (*Continued*)		
#42 Jerome Bettis (*R*)	5.00	20.00
#44 Barry Sanders	3.00	12.00
#77 Steve Young	1.00	4.00
#119 John Elway	1.00	4.00
#124 Brett Favre	2.00	8.00
#142 Dan Marino	3.00	12.00
#146 Drew Bledsoe	4.00	16.00
#151 Thurman Thomas	1.00	4.00
#172 Joe Montana	3.00	12.00
#202 Troy Aikman	3.00	12.00
#218 Garrison Hearst (*R*)	1.00	4.00
Refractors (220)	500.00	2,000.00
#1 Emmitt Smith	50.00	200.00
#172 Joe Montana	50.00	200.00
1994 Upper Deck		
Complete Set (330)	10.00	40.00
Common Player	.05	.10
#7 Marshall Faulk (*R*)	2.00	8.00
#20 Heath Shuler (*R*)	1.50	6.00
#135 Jerome Bettis	.75	3.00
#168 Drew Bledsoe	1.00	4.00
#205 Jerry Rice	.20	1.00
#266 Rick Mirer	1.25	5.00
#277 Troy Aikman	.75	3.00
Pro Bowl Holograms (20)	40.00	160.00
#1 Jerome Bettis	5.00	20.00
#8 Jerry Rice	3.50	14.00
#10 Emmitt Smith	10.00	40.00

SUGGESTED READING

Beckett, James. *The Sport Americana Football Card Price Guide.* Cleveland: Edgewater Book Co., 1994.

Burdick, Jefferson R. *The American Card Catalog.* New York: Nostalgia Press, 1967.

Cosell, Howard. *Cosell.* Chicago: Playboy Press, 1973.

Curran, Bob. *The $400,000 Quarterback.* New York: MacMillan, 1965.

Danzig, Allison. *Oh, How They Played the Game.* New York: MacMillan, 1971.

Erbe, Ron. *The American Premium Guide to Baseball Cards.* Florence, Alabama: Book Americana, 1982.

Gent, Peter. *North Dallas Forty.* New York: Morrow, 1973.

Kaye, Allan, and McKeever, Michael. *The Confident Collector Football Card Price Guide 1995.* New York: Avon Books, 1994.

Kramer, Jerry. *Instant Replay.* New York: New American Library, 1968.

Lazenby, Roland. *The Pictorial History of Football.* New York: Gallery Books, 1987.

Lombardi, Vincent with W. C. Heinz. *Run to Daylight.* New York: Grosset & Dunlap, 1963.

Lombardi, Vincent. *Vince Lombardi on Football, Vols. I and II.* Edited by George L. Flynn. New York: New York Graphic Society, 1973.

Meggysey, Dave. *Out of Their League.* New York: Ramparts Press, 1970.

Namath, Joe Willie. *I Can't Wait Until Tomorrow. . .* New York: Random House, 1969.

Plimpton, George. *Paper Lion.* New York: Harper & Row, 1964.

Rice, Grantland. *The Tumult and the Shouting.* New York: A. S. Barnes, 1954.

Sayers, Gale. *I Am Third.* New York: Viking, 1970.

Shaw, Gary. *Meat on the Hoof.* New York: St. Martin's, 1972.

Thorn, John. *The Armchair Quarterback.* New York: Scribner's, 1982.

Thorn, John. *Pro Football's Ten Greatest Games.* New York: Four Winds, 1981.

Whittingham, Richard. *What a Game They Played.* New York: Harper & Row, 1984.

Zimmerman, Paul. *A Thinking Man's Guide to Pro Football.* New York: Warner Paperback Library, 1972.

INDEX

Italic page numbers indicate a football card on that page.